A CRACK IN THE WALL

A CRACK IN THE WALL

GROWING UP UNDER HITLER

by
Horst Krüger

Translated from the German by
Ruth Hein

FROMM INTERNATIONAL PUBLISHING CORPORATION
NEW YORK, NEW YORK

Originally published in 1966 as *Das zerbrochene Haus*
Copyright © 1966, 1976, Hoffmann und Campe Verlag, Hamburg

Translation Copyright © 1982 by Fromm International Publishing
Corporation, New York, N. Y.

Printed in the United States of America

First U. S. Edition

Library of Congress Cataloging in Publication Data

Krüger, Horst, 1919–
A crack in the wall.

Translation of: Das zerbrochene Haus.
1. Germany—History—1939-1945. 2. Krüger, Horst,
1919–   . 3. Authors, German—20th century—Biography.
I. Title.
DD256.5.K7513   943.086   81-22180
ISBN 0-88064-000-6   AACR2

Of course truth,
struggling with untruth,
must be written,
and it may not be something general,
elevated, ambiguous.
For such general, elevated, ambiguous ways
are precisely the ways of untruth.

—Bertolt Brecht

CONTENTS

A place Like Eichkamp 1

Requiem for Ursula 45

My Friend Vanya 85

In Custody 120

1945: Zero Hour 154

Day of Judgment 190

Afterword: Ten Years Later 234

A CRACK IN THE WALL

A Place Like Eichkamp

Berlin is an endless sea of houses constantly swallowing a torrent of airplanes. It is a vast desert of gray stone, and each time I fly in its direction, I am excited all over again. Magdeburg, Dessau, Brandenburg, Potsdam, the zoo district.

In Berlin they keep busy building subway express lines and inner-city thoroughfares; they devise clever new entry ramps to the superhighway and erect bold television towers. All these go to make up the new, modern Berlin, the technological treadmill of the enclaved city, its circular motion powered internally by the rough, laconic wit of its people and impelled externally by capital.

It is handsome and radiant, this new Berlin, but I do not actually feel at home until I have taken my seat in the interurban train, which these days displays a fair amount of East German shabbiness as it rumbles through the West.

This is my Berlin—the roaring, humming trauma of my childhood, my indestructible iron toy, with its bright, quick clacking that still seems to proclaim, "You're here, you're really here, it's always been this way, this is the way it will remain." Berlin is a hard and shiny bench of polished yellow wood, a dirty, rain-smudged window, a compartment reeking unspeakably of the federal railway system. The odor is a mixture of stale smoke, iron, and the bodies of many workers from Spandau, stuffed with bread and margarine, dragged off to be confirmed at the age of fourteen, daily readers of the tabloids ever since.

Berlin is all this and more. It is a vending machine on the drafty platform, a dispenser of peppermints—white and green tablets wrapped in stiff foil. It is the slamming of the electric doors and the shout at Westkreuz station: "Stay back, please." The shout frightens no one; no one has to stay back these days. But the shout remains, as do the sudden start and the man wielding the signal disc. Berlin is a shabby yellow ticket costing fifty pfennigs. Even today fifty pfennigs lets you ride from Spandau to the capital of the Democratic Republic of Germany.

I am riding the interurban train to get to Eichkamp. I know that Eichkamp is not what we would consider a hot topic these days. Articles on Berlin are in great demand. Give us a piece about the Wall or about the new Philharmonic Concert Hall, the Congress Center, the Christmas preparations over there. There's always a call for that sort of thing.

But Eichkamp? What's that? What is it supposed to mean?

Eichkamp is not listed in any catalogue of Berlin's tourist attractions; no black tribal chief and no American who has crossed the ocean to be enchanted by the glittering shops of the Kurfürstendamm and scandalized by the Wall is taken to Eichkamp. When you come right down to it, Eichkamp is nothing—nothing but a small, insignificant settlement between Neuwestend and Grunewald, no different from the countless other settlements at the edge of the big city, where houses gradually merge with greenery and countryside.

Strictly speaking, Eichkamp is only a memory to me. It is the place of my childhood. It is where I grew up; on its streets I played marbles and king-of-the-hill and hopscotch. It is where I went to school and, later, where I returned from the university to eat and sleep. Eichkamp is, quite simply, my home, and I—a stranger—want to see it again after more than twenty years.

I return as a citizen of the Federal Republic of Germany, leaving behind my profession and my car, my own world. I return alone, but not because I find it stirring and fine that I, a grown man, should try to track down my childhood. Repellent longings of aging men, to wrap themselves around their early years: the obscenity of the old who sit in playgrounds with beating hearts as if there they could discover secret Edens. For me, Eichkamp was not the Garden of Eden, and my childhood was no secret dream. Eichkamp was my youth under Hitler, and I wanted to see it again and to understand once and for all how it was in those days.

More than a generation has passed. Everything that was the Third Reich—the torchlight parades through Berlin's most splendid avenues and the jubilation heard over the radio and the intoxication of renewal—all is gone, past, forgotten. So are the bread coupons and the bombs over Eichkamp and the Gestapo men who sometimes came from the city in black automobiles—all forgotten long ago. By now, I thought, it should be possible to understand. By now almost a lifetime lies between, elation and depression have died away, everything has become new and different. I am a citizen of the Federal Republic, I come from the West, I come to Eichkamp because I am tormented by the question of how it really was, that incomprehensible time. Now, I think, it becomes necessary to understand.

Sometimes at night my dreams lead me back to Eichkamp. They are brooding, anxiety-ridden dreams that awaken me early and leave me feeling broken and battered. Thirty years is a long time. The time of one generation. Time to forget. Why can't I forget?

My dream: I go to Eichkamp, I stand in front

4

of our house. Long cracks snake across the outside walls, for the house was damaged by compressed-air bombs. It is a small two-story row house on the outskirts of Berlin, built cheaply and quickly during the 1920s. Now the damage has been repaired in a slapdash way. The doors and windows are rickety; inside, the wooden floors are splintered.

In the den my mother read aloud to my father. The den was a small, low-ceilinged room furnished in the indescribably discordant way that in those days was called middle-class: department-store junk gussied up with inherited pieces from the good old days. It contained a round table covered with a lace cloth; a floor lamp with a paper shade; a cheap, square pinewood desk studded with brass nails. A chandelier much too large for the space dipped its long crystal lusters deep into the room an heirloom inherited from Buckow. A huge oak wardrobe occupied almost a third of the room: another heirloom; we referred to it as "our baroque wardrobe."

My father, impassive, sat at his black-lacquered desk. As always, he was looking at documents; as always, he scratched his head, his "wound": Verdun, 1916. Behind the table my mother sank down in a cloth-covered spotted armchair; "our club chair," we called it. The lamplight fell gently across the pages. Mother's hands were narrow, her fingers long and delicate, and they flitted nervously over the lines. She had Catholic eyes: dark, believing, goitrously piercing. Her voice had a proclamatory edge. She was reading from a book entitled *Mein Kampf*. It was the late summer of 1933.

No, my parents were never Nazis. It is this fact that makes it seem so strange. As they read from this book by the newly appointed Reich Chancellor, their eyes were large and astonished, like those of children. They read anxiously and expectantly: it must contain fabulous German hopes. They owned no other books, except the city directory for Greater Berlin and the Bible; oh yes, and one novel, popular twenty years before. On New Year's Eve they might go out to hear *Fledermaus*. Sometimes they listened to the radio request program. That was their culture.

My parents were "unpolitical" in the same touching way as almost all the residents of Eichkamp in those days. During the twelve years under Hitler I never actually met a real Nazi in Eichkamp. They were all good, hardworking middle-class families, a little dull, a little narrow-minded, petit bourgeois, the horrors of war and the fear of inflation behind them. Now they wanted peace and quiet. They had moved to Eichkamp at the beginning of the 1920s because it was a new, green island. In Eichkamp pines and firs still stood in the yards, and it was only a quarter of an hour to Teufelssee, where the children could go swimming. They grew vegetables in their gardens. On weekends they were happy to water their lawns. There was almost a smell of open country.

In the city at that time the Roaring Twenties roared along; people danced the Charleston and were beginning to tap-dance. Brecht and Eisenstein were starting their triumphal march. The newspapers reported on street fights in the Wedding district, armed barricades outside the Labor Hall. All that was far away from us, separated as if by centuries—horrible, mysterious cases, breaches of the peace.

In Eichkamp I learned at an early age that a decent German is always unpolitical.

A strange sensation, now that the train is pulling into Eichkamp station. Remembering, forgetting, remembering again; transmutation of time—what is that? What you are doing now is surely not new—you've done it before; it's always been this way. Get up from the yellow polished bench, take your things from the net, push your way past strangers, grasp the brass handle on the door with your thumb pressing on the top, then slowly pull to the right and swing the door open. A feeling of courage.

Now that the train is rushing alongside the platform, step all the way to the front, a sudden wind in your face—and then, while the car is still rolling slowly, the wonderful temptation to jump off. I know it is forbidden; it says so on the sign over the door. It was forbidden under Hitler too. But now I feel the same temptation that took possession of me so irresistibly when I was a schoolboy. If you jump off at just the right instant, and if your feet properly absorb the body's centrifugal force, the momentum will take you up the stairs to Eichkamp, let you be the first at the turnstile, the first outside on the green plaza, the first along the narrow path that leads into town.

The others follow at leisurely intervals. A few men carrying briefcases—inspectors, clerks, civil servants; aging ladies who have been shopping in Charlottenburg or the zoo district and now, a little exhausted, take waddling steps toward tiny houses; young girls visiting an aunt. Young lads with soccer shoes cradled under their arms turn off at the first right because that is the way to the playing fields. In the old days they sometimes wore blue shirts. Those were the Jewish boys, going to the Zionists' athletic grounds.

What is time anyhow? What is there to remember? How is it possible that you are doing all these things again as if you were fourteen? Four years of elementary school in Eichkamp, nine years of attending the Grunewald secondary school. Every day for nine years jumping off the interurban railway, and during that time the swastika over Eichkamp; first skepticism and then elation because things were looking up for everyone after all.

The Katzensteins and the Schicks and the Wittkowskis had moved away. We really hadn't noticed. They were our good Jews; the bad ones lived around the Alexanderplatz in central Berlin. Every resident of Eichkamp had at least one good Jew. My mother favored Jewish doctors. "They are so sensitive," she said.

In those days Arnold Zweig lived in Eichkamp. His fashionably flat roof was un-German; after his escape it had to be gabled in the German manner immediately. Ludwig Marcuse lived three doors from us; he too fled in 1933. None of that was noticed. Right next door to us lived Elisabeth Langgässer. Sometimes she came to our house to listen to the Swiss radio. She always said that in three or four months Hitler would be "done for." She believed it for twelve years. And stayed to the bitter end.

And then the day of the first food coupons. September 1, 1939. I was standing outside the co-op store, and I could no longer buy what my mother wanted. Butter was rationed, bread put on coupons. The good citizens of Eichkamp looked sullen. Wasn't this a repetition of how it had been before, in 1917?

Then the first airplanes. As I stood in the garden, I heard the British engines humming high up in the air. Langgässer stepped to the fence. She was short and stocky, she was rouged to a fare-thee-well, and she wore heavy, horn-rimmed glasses. When she walked down our street, the children behind her shouted, "The paintbox is coming, the paintbox is coming!" And Langgässer said to me, "These are our liberators, Horst, believe me." As she spoke, she stared critically at the sky, blinking, as all shortsighted people do.

And then, later, all the heavy bombs over our area, and the Russians, who also bombed us and also destroyed households and also said, "Woman, come." Did Eichkamp deserve all that? Then the British came, and the years of hunger, the patched-up houses, the time when the black market flourished so luxuriantly. Then currency reform and the airlift. And at last the slow rebirth of the city.

Strange—now Eichkamp is once again what it used to be. It is almost as if nothing had happened, as if all of it had been only an ugly hallucination, a nightmare, an error of history. The error has long since been repaired.

The old row houses remain, a couple of new bungalows are nestled shyly among them. The old houses are narrow and tall, the walls roughcast in yellowish plaster, wild grapes climbing upward along them. The gardens, the gardens of Eichkamp—can this still be Berlin? Thick clusters of lilacs are in bloom again, bluish purple and white; the scent of jasmine wafts from the front yards. Gladiolas, upright as candles, are ranked in beds, and next to them grow strawberries and onions, dill for the kitchen, leaf lettuce, kohlrabi, red cabbage, chervil, and the pines at the rear, the fir trees with their tall, slender, resilient trunks. The radio tower is there as well, and somewhere linden trees are blooming, the linden that figure so prominently in German Romantic poetry; when did I read about them for the first time?

So I am heading for sentimentality. Of course —I am heading home. And as always happens when you go home after years and years, everything gradually grows smaller—the houses, the gardens, the street. How did we manage to live behind such tiny windows? Schmiedt the butcher is still here, selling his sausages and his ground meat; he's got to be as old as Methuselah. And Labude the baker, he's still here too, or at least his shop is. They have endured. I used to go to Labude's to buy Danishes for five pfennigs, and on the weekend I was allowed to buy honeybuns: four at ten pfennigs each. That was our Sunday-morning breakfast cake.

I take the same route I used to take in those days: Fliederweg, Lärchenweg, Buchenweg, Kiefernweg, Vogelherd, Im Eichkamp—all of them

11

narrow, neat streets, still without sidewalks, still lit by gas lanterns, lined by tiny houses with narrow front lawns, green shutters at the old-fashioned windows, and behind them nothing but good, solid citizens who work hard at their crafts, their businesses, their offices. Eichkamp was the world of the good Germans. Their horizons extended just about to the zoo district and to Grunewald, Spandau, and Teufelssee—but no farther. Eichkamp was a small, green microcosm. What did Hitler want here anyway? Here all the votes went to Hindenburg and Hugenberg.

And then, abruptly, I have arrived. But there is nothing to be seen. There is only a hole: rubble, moldering wood, broken stones, a lot of sand, all blanketed in green. A battered suitcase lies below, in the basement. A cellar, decayed, overgrown with weeds, forgotten—a leftover from the war, a dilapidated souvenir of the battle for Berlin, a house in ruins standing cheek by jowl with the gleaming, practical new buildings. Everywhere such empty spaces remain—white dots on the map of our new German affluence. Their owners are dead or missing or living abroad, have forgotten the world of those days and certainly do not wish to be reminded of it.

And I stand and think: But this is your past, this is your heritage, this is the legacy they left you. This is where you grew up. This was your

12

world. The ground plan barely covers thirty square meters. This is where our house stood, two stories high, and on top of that a drafty room for the maids. And it was to these thirty square meters that I was brought in 1923, a three-year-old. The last time I entered this house, in 1944, I was twenty-four, and a German private first class. I was on leave from the Italian front. I brought home a twenty-liter gasoline container. I brought twenty liters of olive oil from Italy, and when we had eaten the hashed-brown potatoes this precious oil made possible once again, all of us were sick. We vomited. The fat was too much. We had to throw up. We—in those days that meant my father, my mother, and myself. My sister had committed suicide long before—in 1938.

So I am back home. I am in Eichkamp. I stand outside our property, the linden trees are in bloom again, and I feel that if I could now understand everything that occurred in this house, I would know how it was in those days—everything about Hitler and the Germans. Somewhere here in the Charlottenburg area there must be a land registry; my name will be inscribed on the title list. It is incontestable. I am still the owner of a ruin, of this ravaged cellar, and if I could only remember, the house would rise again—the colorless, sober, terrible lower-middle-class building of which I am the offspring.

I'm a little ashamed of having come from this narrow, vapid petite bourgeoisie; I would have liked to be the son of an academician or a day laborer. I would have liked to be the son of Thälmann or of Thomas Mann—I'd be somebody, then. But I come merely from Eichkamp. I am the typical child of those innocuous Germans who were never Nazis, and without whom the Nazis would never have been able to do their work. That's how it is.

Remembering, remembering—how can you remember it all? My earliest memory of Hitler is jubilation. I'm sorry about that, because today's historians know better—but I, at first, heard only jubilation. It did not come from Eichkamp. It came from the radio. It came from the distant, foreign city of Berlin, from Unter den Linden and the Brandenburg Gate, which was twenty minutes by interurban train from Eichkamp. That's how far away it was.

It was a cold night in January, and there was a torchlight parade. The radio announcer, whose resonant tones were closer to singing and sobbing than to reporting, was experiencing ineffable events; there seemed to be an indescribable exultation in the Reich capital's street of splendor, where all well-meaning Germans, all genuine and young Germans, had flocked together to pay homage to the aged field marshal and his young chancellor, or so I was told. Both of them were standing at the window. It must have been something like a Hallelujah Chorus of the redeemed: Berlin, a festival; Berlin, a national myth of rebirth. Singing and marching and shouting and surging, and then again the sobbing voice over the radio, chanting something about Germany's awakening, and always adding as a refrain that now everything, everything, would be different and better.

The people of Eichkamp were skeptical. My mother and father listened with astonished and somewhat intimidated ears. It seemed, after all, that such quantities of joy and greatness could not fit into our narrow rooms, rooms already crowded with so much junk and so many old baubles. Soon after eleven my father turned off the radio and, a little perplexed, went to bed. What was happening? What kinds of worlds existed out there?

But the aged marshal and his young chancellor (the latter now frequently in tails), along with those who thenceforth called themselves the Government of National Concentration, finally gathered over Eichkamp, too, like a hope. The skeptics relaxed, those who had been indifferent began to think, the small businessmen grew hopeful. Suddenly over this tiny green oasis of the nonpolitical, the storm of the wide world had broken, not a storm of politics, but a springtime storm, a storm of German rejuvenation. Who wouldn't want to trim his sails for it?

15

The black, white, and red flags of imperial Germany, which the citizens of Eichkamp had always displayed in preference to the black-red-gold ones of the republic, were now joined by Nazi flags, many small and some large, often home-made, with a black swastika on a white ground; in their hurry, some people had sewn the swastika on backwards, but their good intentions were evident just the same.

It was a time of renewal. One day my mother came home with a small triangular pennant and said, "That's for your bicycle. All the boys in Eich-kamp have pretty pennants like this on their bicy-cles now." Like everything she did, this gesture was, of course, unpolitical. It was just that life was so edifying and impressive. In Potsdam the aging marshal and his young chancellor had exchanged a historic handshake: the Garrison Chapel in Pots-dam, the seat of the Hohenzollern, with the old flags and banners of the Prussian regiments flying—everything was very solemn. The ceremony was followed by a grave and gratifying rendition of the song about the good comrade who marched at my side. So my mother went to Hermann Tietz—he was still Jewish—and bought the first swastika pennant.

The Nazis had an infallible knack for provin-cial stage effects. They had all the props to mount a Wagner opera in a suburb, including all the phony magic of the Tree of Life and the Twilight of the Gods, so that the same people who usually listened to light operettas were sent into raptures. Intoxication and rapture are the code words for fascism, for its front, its face, just as terror and death are the code words for its backside; and I believe that the citizens of Eichkamp were eager to give themselves over to intoxication and rapture. They were weaponless. Suddenly one was a somebody, part of a better class of people, on a higher level—a German. Consecration permeated the German nation.

So it came about that in the late summer my mother began to read the book by the new Reich Chancellor. She had always harbored higher aspirations—it was in her blood. She came from an old Silesian family that, somewhat reduced and always in debt, had gradually made its way from Bohemia to Prussia. Like Hitler, my mother was "artistic" and "sort of Catholic." She paid homage to an immensely personal Catholicism: spiritual, wistful, muddled. She was crazy about Rome and the Rhenish carnival; whenever she misplaced her keys, she prayed confidently to Saint Anthony; and occasionally she gave us children a glimpse of the fact that according to her heritage, she was meant for a higher station: membership in the Ursuline order. It was never possible to explain why this nervous and delicate woman, who sometimes gave serious consideration to anthroposophy and vegetarianism, had married the son of a manual laborer from the Starlau district of Berlin. He was not the kind of Protestant who corresponded to her social station, and besides he shared the rude kind of Berlin Protestantism that expresses its faith only in rabid and sneering anti-Catholicism.

My father did not make much of himself in school. His chance came, as it did for so many German males at the time, with the First World War. No, my father was no militarist, he was peaceable and good-natured; but in wartime everything abruptly became plain and simple. He must have been obedient and brave, for as early as 1916 he was seriously wounded outside Verdun. Afterward his career as a modest civil servant went steadily uphill. First the head wound—that was like a stroke of luck; then the Iron Cross, then noncommissioned officer, then sergeant, and finally he must have been something like a second lieutenant; in any case, in 1918 he returned from the war with an officer's sword and a piece of paper that entitled him to begin all over again at the bottom of a "state career." For a time he carried documents; later he pulled a cart along the lengthy corridors of the Prussian ministry of culture; later he was made auxiliary assistant, then assistant, office chief, and finally even inspector.

My father's rise did not end there. By the time

we moved to Eichkamp, he must already have been a chief inspector, a tenured civil servant who could afford to buy a little house, who got a raise and, under Brüning's chancellorship, made it to administrator. For him that was a culmination, a breathtaking pinnacle that enjoined upon him eternal loyalty and submission to the state.

All his life he left home for the ministry at 8:23 A.M., traveling second class. At home he read the old-line newspaper and the local daily, never joined the party, never knew anything about Auschwitz, never subscribed to the *Völkischer Beobachter*, the Nazi party organ—but for twenty minutes, until the train pulled into Friedrichstrasse Station, he held it up before his face so that others might recognize his loyalty to the new people's state. At Friedrichstrasse he left the paper behind. In the ministry, among his trusted cronies, he might sometimes grumble about crude violations of the law by the new leaders. Political jokes were tolerated as well; he especially enjoyed those that began with "Hermann."

All his life he came home at 4:21 P.M., always on the same train, always in the same second-class compartment, if possible always at the same corner window, always holding a briefcase full of work in his right hand, with his left showing his monthly commutation ticket—he never jumped off the moving train. He had achieved his goal; he was a

German civil servant. And no matter whether the government was headed by Noske or Ebert, Scheidemann or Brüning, Papen or Hitler, he was obligated to faith and loyalty. His office was his world, and his heaven was his wife. At that time she was reading *Mein Kampf*, was "sort of Catholic," and was "political" for only a brief period.

I do not know how life actually took its course in the days before Hitler in all those small, angular development houses. I assume that it wasn't very different from life at our house. Get up at six thirty, wash, eat breakfast and put on a cheerful face, go to school, come home to dinner keeping warm in the oven; then homework upstairs, the window open, life beckoning, but back to the books; then my father's return around four thirty, a feeble hope that something would happen—he might have brought something unusual from town. But nothing ever happened at our house; everything was normal, regulated, in order. If it hadn't been for my mother's illnesses—the splendid, adventurous illnesses of a woman full of imagination—my childhood in Eichkamp would have been a single day lasting fifteen years. Fifteen years of nothing, nothing at all that might have been considered high or low, horror or joy; fifteen years of compulsion, of the killing, compulsive neurosis of a faithful civil servant.

Sundays, of course, were always the worst. You had to sleep late because it was Sunday. Sunday 1931 in Eichkamp. Breakfast downstairs dragged on endlessly. My parents' solemn, formal faces because it was Sunday. Monosyllabic exchanges about the condition of the eggs, which were found to be too hard or too soft. Attempts at being friendly, Sundayish, with each other. Attempts to talk about the weather, words that were misunderstood, the beginnings of a quarrel, then silence again. Into the silence the foolish, somehow malicious question whether anyone wanted another cup of coffee. We wore our Sunday best, so that when you poured out coffee, you had to be fiendishly careful.

I had learned at an early age to stare grimly and stiffly out the window during such silences. I always pretended that I wasn't sitting at this family table at all but was somewhere outside, breakfasting all alone amid the greenery, enjoying a magnificent feast of solitude. It must have been a wicked and contemptuous way of ignoring the others. Even at the age of thirteen I was able to spend five minutes vacantly stirring my coffee, devoting my entire attention to a pine tree waving in the wind while my mother and father delivered themselves of terse improvisations concerning the honeybuns, the maid, or the state of our baroque wardrobe. But even my ostentatious absence went unnoticed. In our family nothing was ever noticed. All of us sat like marionettes, unable to reach each other. We dangled from long strings.

After breakfast there were certain high points. My father began to wind our large grandfather clock, which adorned the dining room like a tall, upright coffin. The carved oak was unlocked, the great glass door was solemnly opened, the powerful winding key of heavy brass was fished from the glass-fronted cupboard. Then, abruptly, with a decisive touch of his hand, my father stopped the powerful pendulum. The ticking in the room stopped. Oppressive silence, then the turning and rattling of the gears as the spring was wound in short, taut turns. Dust eddied upward. The procedure was repeated, for the pealing clockwork also had to be retightened. And then my father's power was, so to speak, magically transferred to the machinery. The clock would now tick for another week and ring out its *bim-bam*; the week could begin, Sunday had been secured, the box was closed. Now he lit a cigar that cost twenty pfennigs.

Then followed regular discussions about church attendance. It had been decided in some mysterious way that one of us had to go to church every Sunday. We were not at all religious or devout—but nonetheless. My father was eliminated from consideration, since he was a Protestant, and in Berlin Protestants do not go to church.

My mother always felt a deep need for spiritual comfort, a desire to be surrounded by higher powers—long before Hitler. She expected them to give her consolation and support, felt better when she recalled her days in the convent, but unfortunately the trying state of her health only rarely permitted such pilgrimages. Like almost all women, she frequently suffered from heart trouble; and precisely on Sundays, around eleven o'clock, just when she was about to lay out the fur jacket she had by then acquired, it could easily happen that she was overcome by one of those sudden, unexpected attacks of palpitations. Then we had to run for the drops while she lay down flat on the couch. So it mostly fell to me. Church attendance was simply assigned to the weakest. I was twelve years old, and I wasn't even Catholic. I wasn't Protestant either. I was more or less nothing, like most citizens of Eichkamp. I was the youngest, I couldn't defend myself, and so I was sent to church for the whole family, like the Jews' scapegoat.

Yes, in the years before Hitler that's how it was in Eichkamp—or something like it. At noon there was a universal odor of sauerbraten or calves' head, served with spinach or kohlrabi from the garden. I was always supposed to relate what the priest had said in church. I never really knew, and I proved obstinate. Then my mother became nervous and overly particular; she handled her knife and fork very elegantly and stiffly, poking among her potatoes as though she were using chopsticks. It was as if these elaborate, ritualized gestures would help her to exorcise and dispel the guilt arising from my insufficient faith. Sometimes, even as he tied his napkin around his neck, my father added a scornful remark about Catholics—invariably driving my mother to sit up straight as a ramrod. There was a quarrel. During it, requests to pass the gravy and potatoes continued, and once again I began to pay attention to the world outside the window.

At three o'clock in the afternoon we went to the movies. Children's matinee. Thirty pfennigs for the ticket. I didn't want to go most of the time, but in those days I always had to accompany my sister to the Rivoli in Halensee. Again the empty, meaningless walks through Eichkamp, again moving side by side like puppets having our strings pulled from above. Shortly before Halensee we came upon the state railroad repair works. The way led through a long, dark tunnel—gray, low cement walls, twisting corridors, and suddenly brightness again. A long, somber street, suburban quiet, cobbled pavements, the gutter full of weeds and snippets of paper—an unexpectedly proletarian world.

This was where the railroad workers lived— gray railroad flats, monotonous and vapid tenements, Prussian barracks in the style of 1880, work-worn faces behind the glass of the windows. These were "the Reds," as our mother and father had warned us. I couldn't really imagine anything to go with those words, but you could tell by looking at the Reds that they were dangerous. There must have been a reason, too, why they led their shabby lives here, between Eichkamp and Halensee, in a sort of no-man's-land of Berlin, as if they were behind prison walls. This was the Red rabble—*rabble* was my parents' pet word for everyone who was beneath us: manual laborers and maids, beggars and scissors grinders who rang our doorbell in the mornings, and who of course really wanted to burglarize our house.

At the eastern periphery of Eichkamp, just before the interurban station, lived some more Red rabble. In this area were development houses that had been built recently by the unions, much to the dismay of the older residents of Eichkamp. The cottages were just as shoddy and plain as ours, as alike as two peas in a pod, but my parents always insisted that these were quite different, flimsy and cheaply mass-produced and in no way suited to the sterling style of the old settlers.

It was true that the Reds lived differently. As if to hide the inhabitants, their houses were set far back in the long, narrow strips of gardens. Flower-bordered flagstone paths wavered up to the front doors, and outside you could see chickens running around. Women with washed-out aprons tied around their middles, light-blue kerchiefs on their heads, carried wooden tubs and metal pails back and forth, bustling and keeping busy in the manner of German laborers. A strange, alien world that I never entered, that I beheld with a mixture of curiosity and scorn. For nine years I and my school-books walked past the fences of the Reds. I was, after all, a secondary-school student, destined to be the first in the family to get his diploma. I ventured only searching glances from afar. Distant, forbidden, low world, hope and fear of the bottom—invasion of the Reds in Eichkamp.

Our Eichkamp was something more elevated, more decent. My mother never wore a blue kerchief and no longer carried tubs around; instead she was frequently and extensively ill, and she always spoke of herself as "in poor health," which gave her an aura of communion with higher things. I never did find out exactly what her illness was, but it was why she frequently hired a live-in maid. The maid always smelled of perspiration, was paid thirty marks a month, had fat, spongy upper arms, and after four or five months had to be dismissed "on the spot," as my parents put it. She always became pregnant. When I was a little boy I connected pregnancy with the smell of perspiration. Only later did I hear that "this rabble" was unspeakably filthy and carnal, that they clearly dissipated their Sunday evenings off, notoriously with soldiers, and that in divine punishment, as it were, such waste produced a baby after five months.

They never did explain to me at home all that business about having babies. My parents were not only unpolitical but also unerotic and asexual; maybe the three go together. They were just as silent on the subject of love as they were on the topic of politics. All of it must have been too far beneath them. The sexual stuff had to be especially low and unrefined, for when I finally turned sixteen and, like all the boys of Eichkamp, had long since begun to masturbate, there was a protracted discussion between my mother and father, who must have noticed something. Yes, really, they took notice of something.

One evening I found a thin pamphlet on my nightstand. I was astonished: printed matter had never before played any part in my relations with my parents. I understood at once that something extraordinary had to be involved. I began to read. It was a gentle, mild, amiable piece of enlightenment propaganda beginning with the birds and the bees. Then it talked about the sun and went on to the miracles of God's power, finally making the transition to male power and dealing with the dreaded mortal sins of enervation. These sins were said to be harmful to the spine.

But apparently I couldn't quite follow the argument; it must have been a little too pious for me in those days. It was a Catholic educational tract that my mother, in her perplexity, had acquired from the Ursulines. She never mentioned it, I never mentioned it. We never mentioned this topic at all at home, and if my own body had not become interested in it, I might have managed to reach the age of twenty still believing in the fertile perspiration of our maids. That's the way things were at our house. The German petit bourgeois home barred from its narrow rooms not only the state but also love. The question arises—purely sociologically—what is left to live by when politics and sexuality are gone?

In our case the neighbors were left. There were certain relationships, tentative attempts to approach one's fellow creatures and stake out territory, attempts to break through. On some Sunday afternoons around five thirty, when my sister and I returned from the Rivoli, the Marburgers were in our parlor. They were the neighbors from diagonally across the road. They were rigid, fastidious people whose childlessness added to their refinement. She was tall, he was short, and both wore their Sunday finery, which always gave off a whiff of mothballs. They sat stiff and upright on straight chairs, stirred their coffee with silver spoons, and let fall occasional pointed remarks about the other neighbors. I always felt chilly.

Herr Marburger was also a civil servant who had risen from the ranks, and he was therefore quite evidently my father's peer, but since he was employed merely in the ministry of agriculture, my mother always felt somewhat superior to the Marburgers. On some evenings after the Marburgers had left, there were lengthy debates on the subject, my mother insisting that it made a difference whether one was in charge, like Herr Marburger, merely of cows and forests or, like my father, of art. By this time my father was in fact involved in administering the high school of music in Hardenbergstrasse, and he allowed his wife, who might well have become a singer in the convent, to explain to him that our dealings with the arts put us on an entirely new plateau. That's how fine the distinctions in Eichkamp were in those days.

Sometimes the Stefans paid us a visit. Herr Stefan, it was true, was only a chief inspector—and in the post office, at that. But his oldest son, Oskar, was already in medical school. This lent the Stefans a particularly underhanded form of superiority that they could maliciously use as a trump card by making occasional references to the university and the titillating habits of the fraternity boys. These allusions took my parents aback, and in their turn they were beset by an oppressive sense of inferiority.

This was in the year 1931. The nationwide unemployment figure exceeded four million, a worldwide depression shook the globe; in Berlin the Communists and the storm troopers indulged in bloody street brawls, and one day the banks were closed; and all this time, in the other Berlin, the hectic twenties roared to an end, from the Romanischen Café to the Ullstein Building, while expressionism and the Russian film triumphed.

But my parents took no notice of anything; they were aware only of the excessively fine gradations of rank among Eichkamp society, explaining to me why I was allowed to play with the Naumann children but not the Lehmanns'. The Lehmanns, as it happened, were real academicians, with the letters *Ph.D.* following their name on the plate at the garden gate, and that made them too high for us. My parents had a very clear grasp of "above" and "below." You had to have a feel for it. The people below were rabble, and those above were beyond reach.

The Ernst family, to the left across the road, was equally unattainable; they boasted a doctor and thence derived a multiple superiority. My parents felt honored when the Ernsts said hello, and they were respectful of Dr. Ernst's imposing face, which sported several dueling scars. They never stinted their admiration when they observed the Ernsts' openhanded way of life, which distinguished itself clearly from ours by such luxuries as an occasional taxi ride or the light they left burning over the garden gate at night. And when one day the Ernsts went so far as to buy a car—a little black Opel P4—the event, long before Hitler, was like a small revolution in Eichkamp. My parents watched enviously from behind the curtains as the Ernst family got into this odd vehicle on Sunday afternoons and drove off as if summoned by a higher power. These were obvious signs of their status among the elect.

In those days many of the people of Eichkamp were just like my mother and father: the Nissens and Wessels, Naumanns and Neumanns, the Stefans and Schumanns, Lehmanns and Strübings. All had come from modest backgrounds, all had achieved some small success, all lived in constant fear of backsliding, wanted to stay on top, were somebodies now, proud possessors of that infallible sense for the most minute hierarchical distinctions. They were unpolitical and unerotic, read the local newspaper, did crossword puzzles on Sunday nights, briskly voted for the German National Party, watered their lawns, and set great store by order and convention.

31

Behind our garden lived the Blankenburgers. For a while I was friends with their son Friedrich. Herr Blankenburger was assistant master in a secondary school, and one day I wasn't allowed to go there anymore either. My parents stopped me. It wasn't because he was an educated man—it was worse. On one of their Sunday visits the Marburgers had noted, quite in passing, that Herr Blankenburger was a Red—yes, even he. He was a member of the Social Democratic party, and the old residents of Eichkamp considered the Social Democrats Reds. This was in the summer of 1932.

Thus Hitler's Reich descended on Eichkamp rather like a divine visitation. We had not summoned it, we had not guarded against it. It simply arrived, like a season arrives. The time was ripe. Everything was nature here, nothing was the social order. No one had taken part, no one had been a Nazi. It had all come from distant Berlin, and now it hung like a cloud over Eichkamp: high, with handsome plumage.

The least of our motives was patriotism. I hardly ever heard my parents talk about Germany's defeat in 1918 and the shame of Versailles. The humiliation of Germany never penetrated as far as Eichkamp; it was probably more at home in Potsdam. No, it was not the negative undercurrent of German history that rumbled through Eichkamp. It was simply that everyone was always afraid of backsliding, and now someone had appeared who was eager to carry them ever higher, as on wings. It was just too promising.

Now everything became so wide and large and hopeful. May Day, which was always disturbing to my parents because of the Reds, now became a pleasant holiday in Eichkamp as well, its many flags and chants reminiscent of *The Mastersingers of Nuremberg*. In November the performers from the state opera went through Berlin taking donations for Winter Relief; singers and actors walked along the major avenues carrying red collection boxes.

My mother was unusually animated when she prepared our first one-dish meal, and on that Sunday we all ate the lumpy barley soup in the conviction of having done something for the national community—an altogether new concept for Eichkamp, the national community. Then the block captain stopped by, collected two marks and fifty pfennigs, and gave us a badge. That, too, was a new experience. In addition, a hearty baritone performed over the radio. I think it was Willy Schneider singing the same patriotic folk songs he sings to this day: "Why Is It So Lovely Along the Rhine?" and "Drink a Little Glass of Wine."

This was the new era for us: a little bit of space and graciousness. There was a lot of singing in Germany in those days. The young people were wearing such attractive uniforms, labor service was a good thing—those spades slanting over shoulders made sense to the people of Eichkamp—and now there were so many holidays, all with huge parades and pronouncements. A surge of greatness seemed to course through our country in those days.

Hitler's invasion of our house—35 Im Eichkamp—took place primarily on aesthetic grounds. Beauty—that was it. The man was an artist, after all, an architect and painter, and in his youth in Vienna he had "asserted his inner self," as my mother put it. She understood this sort of thing, but of course she meant it more morally than politically: she too had always wanted to become an artist. And now he was erecting opera houses and art galleries everywhere, tearing down half of Berlin, planning everything on a large scale, designing splendid new ministries and a Reich Chancellery that on the outside looked like a Greek temple, drawing arrow-straight roads through the landscape: it gave my mother physical pleasure.

At that time she joined the Nazi Cultural Association; that way you could get a discount when you went to see *Fledermaus* or see Emmi Sonnemann who had made it at the side of her powerful husband, Göring. All Germans were making it now. And the music—wonderful German music—and the art! Now we had real confirmation that art was more important than agriculture, and an administrator in the ministry of culture was higher than one in the ministry of agriculture. The new era was, simply, "artistic"—that was my mother's favorite word in those days.

I can remember the first day of our summer vacation in 1934. A hot July morning. We had taken our seats in the vacation train to Hirschberg, which was still standing at the Schlesische Railroad Station. My mother was wearing a dress patterned with large flowers; she was surrounded by suitcases and bags, and food was being spread out. My father entered the compartment holding a morning paper. Big banner headlines. He read. They talked to each other, their faces serious as they whispered. Suddenly a stricken look came over their features. There was talk of sexuality and of something else preceding that word. I didn't understand, but I heard that it would be better to try "that kind" before a proper court, not simply shoot them down in bed. This procedure aroused my father's disapproval. These were the first clouds on our vacation sky.

I remember the morning after Crystal Night, in November 1938. Tauentzienstrasse was littered with splintered glass from the broken display windows of the Jewish stores, and storm troopers with shoulder straps stood by and observed the passersby. We walked past in embarrassment and silence. That night my father told us that synagogues had been burned and the "rabble"—he said "rabble" again—had looted Jewish stores and apartments. Thoughtful faces at home, silent indignation: Does the Führer know about this?

My mother had her private worries about the man. She was, after all, a Catholic, and the Concordat must have given her deep satisfaction, but later there were pastoral letters that were read from the pulpit and tended to make you think. The papers did report such a lot about convents and monasteries. Every day the police, searching for currency criminals, discovered evil practices concealed by pious habits. There was talk of pederasty— I still didn't understand that part fully—but it scared my mother that of all people the Franciscans, whom she esteemed so deeply, could be so depraved. Still later there were other pastoral letters that earnestly and prudently professed support for the people's state but then moved on to discuss euthanasia, which they said was to be repudiated. It was a dilemma for my mother: on the one hand she fervently revered the clergy, on the other her "artistic" side drew her to the new Reich. It was the old conflict between ethics and aesthetics—Kierkegaard's invasion of Eichkamp.

But such meditative moments could not hide the fact that we were living in a new and great era. The Reich and youth, art and the state—only now did it become clear in Eichkamp what forces these were. Everything was suddenly so solemn: Beethoven concerts on the radio preceded the Führer's speeches; the great man himself went to Bayreuth in all humility; statues of naked youths hailed us from post offices, holding aloft blazing torches— Greek springtime in Germany. True, no one from Eichkamp had ever visited Greece.

They were just about to build the huge stadium in Heerstrasse for the 1936 Olympic games, and a reflection of greatness fell even on Eichkamp. There, right next to the railroad station, they built the largest assembly hall in the world, the huge ceiling entirely without supporting pillars. Our small, sleepy depot was now called Germany Hall and had an exit at the rear exclusively for visitors. That elevated us a little more.

Actually so much greatness stood in peculiar, bizarre contrast to our little settlement, but when I think about it, that was exactly what made it so fascinating. The people of Eichkamp were not used to such dimensions. They were left disarmed, willing, and docile. They were like children, were simply ecstatic to hear what a great thing it was to be a German, to see this Germany becoming ever greater and greater.

And the Reich certainly was growing daily. Everything got better and better, everything rose higher and higher, and since the residents of Eichkamp really did come from the bottom, they were perfectly willing to be swept aloft by these successive waves of elation. Life was, after all, on the upswing. Why not? Herr Berger said, "Finally we're having our turn on the stage of world history—it's only fair." Herr Stefan said, "Now we have highways, so our mail will move even faster." Frau Marburger said, "We'll adopt a child now that so many German mothers are having babies." Herr Schumann said, "And our colonies, we'll get them back now, too—that's obvious," and he went to the attic in search of his old sou'wester. And Herr Nissen even had hopes for the Kaiser: "The Hohenzollern, they're coming back. Somebody's been to Doorn already to talk to Wilhelm. You'll see."

One day, shortly after Austria was annexed to the Reich, I met Frau Stefan in the street. I was coming home from school. She said, "What, you don't believe that the Führer was sent to us by God?" I had no idea that Frau Stefan was so devout, such a believer. Her husband, after all, was merely a postal employee. But apparently this was another thing it took Hitler to bring to Eichkamp: the knowledge that there was such a thing as Providence, divine justice, and a Lord. Even in Eichkamp these invisible powers were mentioned a lot now.

It was a reverential time indeed. My mother had cut out one of the Führer's sayings for which she felt an ambiguous admiration. She wanted to discuss it with me. The man had said, "By opposing the Jews, I am doing the Lord's work." They said something very like that in church—didn't they? She repeatedly sought clarification of this statement, first from the clergy, then from me. She tried to understand anti-Semitism on a higher, theological plane.

What I mean to say is: in those days—the autumn of 1938—everything in our world took place on a higher plane. Hitler and Eichkamp were way at the top then. Devoutness covered all the land.

Yes, unless my memory fails me, that's more or less how it was for us in those days. I know it is offensive to dig up such memories today. It's a little embarrassing and ludicrous, and nobody is any longer willing to admit to involvement in such fervent and childish displays. Today our country is swarming with resistance fighters, secret agents, men who went into "inner emigration," and sly foxes who only pretended to go along in order to prevent worse. The German people—a people of resistance fighters. The German people —a people who were all persecuted. Oh, if only there hadn't been the storm troops and the Gestapo, these people would have risen up against Hitler. It was just that they couldn't.

These are the new myths of the present day, the current bright lies of our historians, all of whom relieve us of our burden so pleasantly with their neo-German accounts of historical events. They make everything so intelligible—brown terror over Germany—all except one point: why the Germans loved this man, why they honestly rejoiced at his coming, why they died for him by the millions. Just look at the military cemeteries all over the world. These dead were not, as they are today in East Germany, uniformed men backed up by still more uniformed and armed men. They were honest believers, enthusiasts, inebriates; in those days they practically begged for a hero's death. The only fear was of being late to the victories. And in 1938, if someone had raised his hand to fire the fatal shot at Hitler, there would have been no need of storm troopers or Gestapo to catch him. The people themselves would have sentenced and condemned him, the killer of the Messiah. That was how it was.

And yet—they were never Nazis. The Nazis proper really had come out of nowhere; they were at most five percent of the population, people who had never learned a trade, were not skilled at anything, were born losers. And they certainly would

40

have been "gotten rid of" again after three or four months if only all the good and decent Germans in Eichkamp had not blindly put at their disposal all the native energy, industriousness, faith, and skills they possessed. Thus they slowly stumbled from their lower-middle-class dream into an era of greatness. Now they felt wonderful, were enormously proud of what the man had made of them. They never understood that it was they—all of them together—who had first made the man. Without them he would never have been able to make his way out of the back room of the Hofbräuhaus. To the end they always thought they owed it all to Hitler: the era of greatness and the era of death.

My parents, too, believed to the end. October 1944. What did it was the business about the olive oil from Italy, a domestic crisis that happened to coincide with the disaster of history. I came from the front; I hadn't seen my family for four years. They had become frighteningly old; for four years of war they had lived in Eichkamp exclusively off ration coupons, and now even their expressions were exhausted, rationed. They were like addicts suffering abrupt withdrawal from morphine: shaky and collapsed. My mother, who all through the years of greatness had dyed her hair a handsome black, had now turned snow-white and was genuinely devout—I suspected even then that the

41

churches in our country could not help but experience a great boom after Hitler; there was such a lot of disillusioned devotion. And my father, who had never understood these worshipful attitudes, no longer understood anything at all, was at his wits' end, just kept shaking his head; his neck strangely spindly and leathery jutted from the wide collar. All he did was moan softly, "The bastards, the criminals, what have they done to us! After the war, we'll all be carted off to Russia, that's quite obvious." Actually there was no need for him to reproach himself. He had never joined the party. His denazification questionnaire would be splendid, clean as a whistle.

Interurban station, Eichkamp. October 30, 1944. The Russians in Silesia, the Americans in the Ardennes. End of my leave. They came with me to the train. It was drafty on the cold, empty platform. They stood there, black overcoats flapping along their skinny bodies, weakness, hunger, fear were in their faces. Some sort of love, without an object, haunted their eyes; weariness showed between the wrinkles. Dying petit bourgeoisie telling itself one last lie. Everyday conversation— "You'll always be one of us"; embarrassed laughter; my mother's anxious speeches about how I was to behave at the front—dress warmly always, never go too far forward, always do only what the others are doing; reassurances that we would soon meet again, under happier circumstances. The train pulled in. I picked up my luggage. I was twenty-four years old, they were almost sixty. I felt strong, they were ancient in their tremulous helplessness. Familiar embrace, awkward. I got into the interurban train, closed the door, went to the window. I opened it and leaned out.

So there they stood, outside, the people who brought me into the world: parents of Eichkamp. They seemed slightly absurd in their impotence; I almost wanted to laugh, but I felt more like crying. Now they were waving their handkerchiefs, growing smaller and smaller; now they looked almost like Philemon and Baucis. I knew that I would never see them again. Never. This was the end, their death. The Russians would come, their son was gone. "You're all we've got. You'll stay with us. You're all we've got left. They've taken everything away from us, my God. You are our hope"— that's what they clung to. Another illusion; they had always lived on illusions.

This was how it would happen. They would fall ill, lie alone somewhere, die alone, the Russians among them. The funeral would be a disgrace. There were so many dead bodies in Berlin in those days. There was an epidemic of suicides. There were hardly any coffins left, and wood was in short supply. Yes, you'll be stuck in paper bags, like vegetables in paper bags—that's what you'll get from your Hitler—and be buried hurriedly some-where along the Wannsee.

But as yet they were still here. They were tiny black dots now, still clinging to me, reluctant to let go—my parents. They did not stop waving: That's right, isn't it? You'll never leave us?

I had long since disappeared. My throat chok-ing, I threw myself on the bench of polished yellow wood, and my gas mask thumped. I thought, Thank God that's over. You'll never see them again. You've finished with all that. Never again will you return to Eichkamp—never again.

Requiem for Ursula

I ride on the interurban train for a long time. From Eichkamp to Priesterweg it takes almost three-quarters of an hour. After that, the landscape becomes open and empty. The city dissolves. The air is damp and muggy. Signals stand dripping in the fog. Forgotten names of streets and districts fly past the window—unexplored precincts when I was a child, not explored even yet. Berlin is part of the East. The people of Berlin have names that hail from Silesia and the Baltic, from the Danube and the Oder. I never noticed until I returned from the West after the country was divided. They have pale, sleepy faces with Wendish cheekbones and narrow, colorless lips. And when they sit across from me here on the interurban railway—wearing trousers that are somewhat too loose and coats that are a little too long, some of the women with kerchiefs around their heads—and when it grows dark at three o'clock in the afternoon, then who can tell me, here in the dusk just outside Berlin, that I am not headed for Cracow or Warsaw? Berlin is very Eastern.

At Priesterweg Station, no one else gets off. The platform is high and narrow and drafty, and everything made of iron looks rusted. There is a smell of November in the air. The eye roams freely over damp fields, allotment gardens with arbors made of roofing felt, beer bottles still lying around from the summer, spades, tin cans, reddish-brown flowerpots. A water tower stands between the gardens commandingly, like a cement mushroom; a coal dealer's shop comes next. Stairs, corridors, a tunnel—why are railroad underpasses in Berlin always so bare, so high, and so drafty? I can hear my steps echoing back from the walls. There is the whistle of a locomotive and the sound of signals striking somewhere overhead. A small freight cab rattles by on three wheels, laden with old-fashioned furniture perhaps belonging to a pensioner moving to the south end of Berlin. And then, just before the cemeteries, nurseries with flowers for the dead and iron wreaths on the fence: stands of pious mortality. "Mourning Accessories of Every Description," I read. Then the workshops of the stonemasons, where impressive palm fronds are chiseled in marble and blank slabs stand waiting for names. Sometimes a coffin dealer as well. The shopwindow displays his wares—carved wood, polished brown, open-lidded, inviting you to a resplendent end.

I have missed it for a long time. I should have

come here years ago. The road from Frankfurt to the south end is long. If you happen to come to Berlin, you have time for quick trips to the zoo, the Hansa section, and the Messedamm—you always avoid cemeteries. I have not been back here for three years, and I'm filled with a kind of worry and a bad conscience. There are obligations that cannot be ignored. Even if in life we do not meet, in death we are oddly united. They say the grave serves as a reminder. But maybe the truth is only that graves are tough as scars; they stir up ancient history. Like old folks, they always tell the same stories, monotonous, boring, accusing; no one wants to hear them. The language of the grave is the language of the pensioner: that's how it was, it won't ever be the same again; that was life.

The last survivor must learn this language. The whole burden of memory rests on him.

I carry within myself the weight of three people who were once alive. I barely knew them, but they live in me now and will die only with me. That's what is meant by family, Eichkamp family —it's so long ago. In me it all comes together, and if I were a decent person, I would pack up and move to Berlin, I would visit their graves regularly.

The last survivor is always something like a cemetery custodian. His life consists entirely of acts of rememberance and of devotional preservation. I do not like that duty, I do not want it. When I come to Berlin, I'm looking for life. I wander to the zoo and to Hardenbergstrasse, I ride to Moabit and taste the odors of Spandau and Halensee, the minute distinctions between Schöneberg and Charlottenburg. And everywhere I still expect something wonderful. That's how it happens that I have not come to the cemetery for three years.

Red-brick building from the 1880s, Wilhelminian severity, Prussian air in the corridors, cardboard signs along the walls—Cemetery Regulations, Visiting Hours, Resolutions of the Magistrate and the Community—the church, a communal burial association. A tiny, wizened man crouches behind a wooden barrier, turning the pages of heavy ledgers. He leafs through the years of the dead as if they were living, secret troops under his command, present to him in the graveyard, as real as soldiers in an orderly room. And I say, "Yes, her name was Ursula K. She was buried here in '38, early in April. I visited her here often. She was my sister."

The custodian takes great pains. As always in Prussia, everything is registered and ordered, and it really should be a matter of moments and a couple of references to find any corpse. I need only ask the number of her grave, because it's so easy to get lost among the tombstones. The dead all bear an uncanny resemblance, and nothing is more embarrassing than to find youself grieving at the wrong marker. But today the process seems fraught with difficulty. "In '38?" the old man asks. "April '38?" And he takes still other ledgers from the shelf, dampens his index finger on a green sponge, and continues to leaf through his yellowed forest of the dead.

There is much noise in the room. The sere pages rustle like parchment when they are turned, and the crackle of the fire can be heard from the little potbellied stove. The room is warm; in Berlin they take heating seriously, I think to myself. As in Vilna and Leningrad, they are determined here to fire up mightily against the winter. I begin to unbutton my coat and my jacket. "I'm going," I say. "I'll manage to find it—I've been here many times."

But the little custodian had sunk his teeth into the problem, has scented a case, has taken on a serious responsibility; something that is not in his records—how can it be outside in the graveyard? The search continues for a quarter of an hour or more as all sorts of registers and files are consulted and thick folders from the prewar years are examined. It seems grotesquely clear that one dead person in Prussia's keeping has been lost. Nothing of the sort has ever happened in Berlin before.

Finally the old man looks up, sudden enlightenment written on his features. He lays his finger against his temple and asks, quick as a wink, "Did you say April '38? Did you say Ursula K.? Of course," he continues, "the row of graves in Section S." He reaches for another oblong ledger, eagerly turns the pages of his book of the dead, consults still other lists. Abruptly his whole face lights up—a custodian's joy, wonderful to see. "We've got it!" he shouts, jumps up from his office stool, and eagerly drags all the documents over to where I stand. He is blissfully happy, and as he runs a pencil down a list, he says triumphantly, "It doesn't exist anymore. It's gone—I mean the grave. We leveled it last year."

And to my astonishment I discover that graves, like people, can die; yes, it can happen. You might come home to find that your wife is dead; in the same way, years later, you might come to a grave and find it gone. The grave itself has died, and nothing is left, nothing at all. I learn with horror that two years ago the twenty-five-year burial period expired. For more than a year a notice had been pinned up in the hall out there, for more than a year they had tried to warn the family, who could not be reached any other way, to buy up the same plot again. Otherwise it would be obliterated and another corpse would be billeted there; earth is in short supply. No one came all that time, no one was willing to renew the grave, and so this past January—"Wait," said the old man, "I can tell you exactly, if you're interested. A Franziska

Busch is now occupying the place where your dear sister used to be."

My dear sister—for a moment I am overcome with fright and numbness. Guilt engulfs me, paralyzing fear of the annihilation that has occurred: she is gone. Surely that's not possible, it can't be. They had been looking for me, to tell me, and I didn't come.

Just leveled it, just laid someone else in it—imagine something like that being allowed. They can't take our dead away from us too, can they? I always thought to myself, The cemetery, there's time for that, it won't run away. Now I am told the grave no longer exists; my sister has been wiped out of the world, and to be fair, I am the one who killed her. So that is guilt; now I know how it feels. I have destroyed her grave—an ancient taboo, of course, like incest or matricide. Now it awakens, the ancient guilt. Nothing is left of her—she lives only in me. In me it all comes together. If I do not remember now, she will be dead forever. So I will have to remember.

Austria had just returned home to the Reich. Eichkamp's air was still saturated with Greater German rejoicing, much Viennese gratitude. The world spirit was marching through our country in those days; history was happening at our own front door. Our front door was painted green, was made of pinewood, and had just been given its first safety lock and chain—because of burglars.

It was March 1938. Germany's affairs were going very well then, but we were not among those who enjoy thrusting themselves forward during such times. The pushy ones are all alike— and, as we know, not the best kind of people. Bluster was not our way. In many middle-class homes Greater German rejoicing ended thought-fully; in Eichkamp, Greater German shouting quietly turned into loyalty. In those days we must have been something like a decent German family, one among many millions who thankfully and zealously took part in the rapid rise of our people.

The evening had passed like any other Sunday evening at our house. We ate supper: bologna sandwiches and cheese sandwiches washed down with beer, two tall, narrow bottles of a special Berlin brand. We listened to the radio, looked through the local paper, stopped at the crossword puzzle. My mother happily embroidered some flowery thing. My father looked through his files and puffed blue smoke clouds around his head.

Around nine o'clock it was my mother's cus-tom to supply herself with books and medicine and retire upstairs to her bedroom. Lately she liked to read such thinkers as Coué and Rudolf Steiner, and she occupied herself very earnestly with the advantages of vegetarianism. The word was out in those days that even the great man in the Reich Chancellery had been able to achieve his marvelous successes only by giving up meat. The genius fed on a vegetarian diet. Mysterious associations seemed to be at work here, and my mother always wanted to get to the bottom of them.

At ten o'clock my father listened to the news. There were reports from all over the world, felicitations, good wishes, many assurances of loyalty —and not just from Germany. Then, ten minutes after ten, my father went to bed. I had long since gone to my room and was lying in bed listening to him shuffle through the hall and downstairs to the cellar, where the water and gas mains had to be turned off. My mother always insisted that the main cock of the gas pipe had to be firmly locked and the key placed on her nightstand. The large, slightly rusted square key lay next to a volume of sermons, and both gave us a strange sense of security.

I heard my father come up the stairs, heard him lock the bedroom door twice from the inside, heard my parents' monosyllabic exchanges, heard my father unlock the wardrobe and drop his high boots, and heard the bed creak. I lay next to my colorfully worked wall hanging, a fake Persian rug that came from Wertheim's department store and gave rise to wonderful fantasies. I always tried to follow the convoluted labyrinth, the intricate paths between red and black, to discover the secrets of the Orient. In the process, I fell asleep. Dreamlike figures pursued me. Eichkamp began to sleep now and to breathe deeply. All of Eichkamp dreamed calmly and expansively on its way to Germany's future.

The following morning a cry awoke me. I heard blows, the splintering of pinewood. My alarm clock read eight thirty. There was a wild uproar, horror, as if a civil servant had incomprehensibly overslept by half an hour. I burst out into the hall in my pajamas. My feet were bare, something my father had always forbidden because I might catch cold. But now no one cared.

Her door was broken open; the lock, surrounded by fractured wood, still stuck in the frame; the wood was fibrous and yellow; the door dangled oddly askew on the hinges. Her window had been thrown open, pale spring light covered the world outside, and Ursula lay in bed—it was as if I were seeing her for the first time. She lay stiff and white on the coverlet, her hands folded as if in prayer, her brown hair falling softly over the pillow. She lay beautiful and alluring, like a department store mannequin, and a dark-red, almost black thread trickled down from the left corner of her mouth over the white skin to the pillow and there, on the clean linen, formed a large stain.

It was as if I recognized the whole scene. It was almost like an opera by Puccini, the fourth act, Mimi's death—my God, how often we had seen it at the German State Opera. Red dancing slippers lay on their sides, a white ballgown was thrown across a chair, and various bits of underclothing, pale and pink, were scattered girlishly over the floor. Beside a piece of lingerie lay a yellow glass tube, which I picked up. It frightened me. The inscription was flanked by two huge skulls such as I had until then seen only on the visored caps of the storm troopers. Each skull stared at me menacingly from two black eye sockets; behind them two bones were crossed, and between them, with two exclamation points, it said, "Warning, Poison!!" and I read the word *sublimate*, which meant nothing to me.

Ursula was not dead. She was weeping. A soft, suppressed whimper escaped her clenched lips, and once when she tried to open her mouth, black blood gushed out and formed a thick clump on the white pillow. She closed her lips again immediately.

I felt a strange sense of calm and agreement: I was possessed by clarity. I was nineteen years old, was working toward my diploma, and knew, like all nineteen-year-olds, much more than my parents. I had heard a thing or two about Homer and Socrates, had learned in school about the great deeds of the ancient Germanic people and Tacitus' song of praise, and all that now gave me a surprising superiority of understanding. I grasped the situation in an instant, and I thought, Of course; such things are possible. And why not kill oneself? It's always in the air. I understand you, you needn't tell me anything, just close your mouth tightly; otherwise the blood will spurt, and then it will be like a Puccini opera. Please don't start on arias of self-pity—I can't bear them. Mother sounded them out so often on the piano in the parlor: Verdi's *Otello* in the fourth act, the last act of *Traviata*, the final duet of *Aida*—now the tomb has enfolded them forever. We know all that in this house. Here one always dies in the last act; it's a requirement of Eichkamp dramaturgy.

None of us managed a sensible word. My mother cried out from time to time and uttered shrill sounds of despair, and my father ran around the tiny room helplessly, excitedly, explaining categorically that she had done this to him, to him alone. It was an attempt on his life. I'm certain he had never read Freud and had no idea what the Oedipus complex was, nor had he ever heard of Electra, and yet he quite correctly related the situation directly to himself.

There was a kind of primal shock and primal memory in us, a strange moment of truth at the center of the intoxication about the return of Austria, and I thought, You lie there like a mannequin, but you are like a man; you have displayed courage. I envy you, Ursula; you got out of this German opera, which we saw so often in Charlottenburg. The last-act props are strewn around carelessly, the character actors are now singing the required refrains of horror, and soon the chorus will draw the moral balance sheet: That's how it is, that is the world, that was her life; so it is written everywhere. The last survivor must laboriously learn this language.

Suddenly I felt something like love. The fact that you did this brought me close to you. You were my sister, there was no denying it, but did we every pay attention? Blood relationships are a strange matter. The blood in our bodies stays there and cannot bind us. Only when it leaves us, Ursula, does it bind us. Your blood is my blood; at this moment you are becoming my sister. We always walked side by side to the Rivoli, to the zoo, to Grunewald, to the state opera. I did not know what went on inside you. And what did you know about me? We walked alongside each other like puppets on long strings. We did not know one another—how should family members know one another? Family is coldness, strangeness, ice; no one member can touch any of the others. Family words are formulas, and family conversations are petrified misunderstandings: Yes and no and please and thank-you and what do you want, what do you think, what did you say, yes, please, yes, I'm coming, hurry up, what's the matter, right away, just wait, we're here, and how are things at home? We often exchanged these formulas among ourselves, and we remained deaf all the same. Only now do I understand you. You are my sister. In death we are oddly united.

This particular Monday morning in March 1938 turned into a strange and, as it were, musical commotion at our house. Never have I felt as much at home in Eichkamp as in the days when Ursula was dying. A dam had burst, a wall had collapsed; all at once life came to our house— marvelous, wild life, wonderful unrest—and nothing went as it should any longer. Chaos broke in. At our house everything had always run its automatic course, had gone like clockwork: sleeping, rising, breakfast, the schoolbooks, and the walk to the Eichkamp railway station—my pocket invariably held the yellow commutation ticket. I always longed for something extraordinary and wonderful: a summer day spent at Teufelssee and many naked men and so much sorrow in me. It must have been life I was looking for, and now it had suddenly arrived. Its name was Chaos.

My parents were no match for such afflictions. They ran around in despair and perplexity, breathlessly climbed the stairs and, muttering unintelligibly, went back down again, threw open the windows and shut them again, closed the curtains in one room and pulled them apart in the next. Sometimes my mother collapsed in exhaustion and fell into her club chair. She complained out loud, then began to weep softly; later her weeping turned into prayer. From the den you could hear a beseeching Our Father and a higher and more rapidly intoned Hail Mary. Meanwhile my father, who had never aspired to higher connections, was forced to look for the key ring, which had been misplaced in all the excitement.

And of course both of them were confronted by an enigma, a puzzle. It was much worse and harder to understand than the events of seven years later, when we were once more afflicted, when in another March—1945—British bombers used compressed-air bombs to turn our house into rubble forevermore. This, now, must have been something like a preliminary tremor at the heart of the home, an intimate vibration of world history. When things took on clear political outlines, they became almost comprehensible again. But the family circle is beyond the rational. Family is a puzzle.

My parents bemoaned their fate, which had taken such an unfortunate turn. They spoke of the bosom of the family and of the ingratitude of children, and they listed their good deeds during the World War, during the inflation, during the depression. There had always been milk in the house, even in 1923, and all the schoolbooks had been bought, and then there was the money for summer camp and the whole burden of raising children. Everything had always turned out well, everywhere things were looking up, and this was the thanks you got—just throwing life away like that, as if it were nothing.

They agreed on this point—that Ursula's decision not to live any longer was an act of extraordinary ingratitude. It was a revolt against God's order according to my mother, a revolt against the state according to my father, and in both cases it signified a sinful lack of gratitude and was at bottom directed exclusively against her parents. Children owe their parents everlasting, inexhaustible gratitude, and children who kill themselves actually kill their parents, I was told. There seemed to be some truth to this final conclusion.

On this particular Monday morning my parents could consider themselves lucky that they had me. In their desperation they would have left Ursula lying there all day. They were so intensely occupied with their misfortune that they were not equipped to cope with crisis. So I had to handle the situation. I felt nothing but coldness and clarity. I was nineteen years old, and yet I acted with the level-headedness of a fifty-year-old: my mind was stone sober. I stood on the firm ground of truth, and I told myself, Now you must get the telephone book, look under *Emergency* or *Hospital*, pick up the receiver, say something about an accident, and summon an ambulance. She must be attended to at once; perhaps she can still be saved. You'll have to start to care about your sister—this is the first chance you've had.

Of course the entire matter had to be hushed up. When the ambulance came to the door and the men with their black bags and the long cloth stretcher clattered up our steep stairs, my mother rushed out into the street, where people had gathered around the car marked with the red cross. Such vehicles from the emergency station only rarely found their way to Eichkamp, and one could be sure that something extraordinary was in the offing.

Once, in 1929, in Lärchenweg—I must have been nine or ten years old—an elderly spinster had taken poison. It must have been gas, for the firemen clumsily scaled ladders along the walls, performed elaborate gymnastics on the roof, and from there climbed down through some opening or other. I did not understand what was happening—nothing could be seen from the outside, and everything looked as it always did. But my mother had been afraid of gas ever since, and the business with the square cellar key stemmed from that episode. Once a married couple had committed suicide with sleeping pills; that was in 1934. It was said that they were Jews, and something so horrible seemed somehow characteristic of Jews. Once a maid from Kiefernweg had strangled her illegitimate baby with a towel. The news spread like wildfire through our little settlement, irrefutably confirming the complete depravity of the lower orders. My mother even fired the maid we had at the time because she scented danger to her children. She always said, "They're all the same, one rabble like another. They've all been marked by God."

Yes—and now it was our turn. Now the ambulance was parked in front of our house at 35 Im Eichkamp. It was the spring of 1938, the world was still in one piece, our house looked attractive and inviting, the walls were covered with wild grapes, and pansies were beginning to sprout in the front yard. And while the men upstairs moved my whimpering sister to the stretcher, my mother downstairs explained to the people in the street that we were dealing with appendicitis—a case of acute, morbid infection of her daughter's appendix. That made sense, so then she ran upstairs and for the first time carefully wiped the blood from her daughter's face, for naturally even the people of Eichkamp were aware that appendicitis victims did not generally bleed from the mouth.

Then the ambulance drove off. No one was allowed to ride along. The medics had understood the circumstances at once and perhaps suspected an illegal action; they said that everything must be left as it was and that they would have to notify the police. Our green door of pinewood fell shut, the new safety lock clicked audibly, and suddenly I and my parents were trapped like mice. Eichkamp imprisonment—now it took on reality. A semblance of crime, an aura of greatness and destiny, clothed us. Perplexed, we sat in our large club chairs and for the first time felt the breath of the great world drift through our narrow rooms. Life was incomprehensible—who would have expected this? Gone were school, the Hitler Youth, and the worthy teachings of Tacitus concerning the Germanic people; gone were the ministry, Education Minister Rust, and many good laws and regulations of the people's state; gone all the art about which my mother was so enthusiastic, Schubert's *Winterreise* and Wagner's Wesendonk lieder. Abruptly death had entered, and we were no match for it.

We sat as if time had stopped. On that morning we were like bad amateur actors performing sloppily improvised versions of *Electra* and *Antigone* in a Berlin back room. Tragedy had moved in with us, and of course we were hardly equal to such scripts. I was especially bad in my part. I should have been moved and grieving. The role demanded no less; she was my sister. But all I felt was an evil sensation of triumph: There you have it. Finally it has come out. This is life, and only this.

Ursula was taken to the Westend Hospital. For twenty-one days, tough and determined, she lived on, resisting the end she had summoned. Death rose slowly from her nether regions, beginning between her sex and her intestines and creeping upward little by little. It was a case of rabid poisoning, as the doctors explained to us.

Sublimate is highly concentrated mercury, and anyone who swallows a sufficient quantity releases the poison into the stomach and thence into the intestines. There it comes to rest and begins its murderous task of dissolution. Sublimate destroys all living matter, corrodes the tissues; it makes gruel of our flesh and very slowly turns our organs into a bloody pulp. The disintegration rises, and when it reaches the kidneys, it turns them to mush. Since they can no longer eliminate urine, the fluid accumulates in the body; when it reaches the heart, the heart stops. And that is the end. The condition is called uremia, and most of the time it progresses very quickly; only in Ursula's case did it take so long. She lingered for three weeks, and these three weeks gave us an opportunity to comprehend our misfortune gradually, to come to terms with our catastrophe. Death requires style, and style needs to be developed. Who could comprehend death without style?

The shadow of criminality had quickly fled from our house. My father telephoned the police from his ministry, the Westend Hospital telephoned my father, and then the police telephoned the Westend Hospital. The matter was now running in official channels, which quickly and completely exonerated us. The story about the appendicitis, it is true, could not be kept up for long in Eichkamp. Some bits and pieces had seeped out, and admissions had to be made, at first vague and ambiguous; one had to make adjustments. My mother spoke more frequently now of the facts that had afflicted us, and when one day at dinner she suddenly confessed, "The poor child, our Ursi, what she must have suffered," she had found the right approach.

Slowly life at our house straightened out again. The everyday world claimed its rights. I went back to school, prepared for my diploma exam, wrote a long term paper about Hans Grimm and the people's *lebensraum*. My father once more took the 8:23 train to the ministry of culture and brought home many files concerning art, and my mother's cooking, performed with greater concentration, was more tasty than before. And in the afternoons we took turns going to the Westend Hospital to visit our mortal child—not such a child: twenty-one years old. It was a stirring enlargement of the familial *lebensraum*. We had never gone beyond the confines of Eichkamp so frequently. True, something was now missing at home, but in return we had a high and bright room in Charlottenburg from which the tremors of another world clearly emanated. We rode the interurban train, but our journeys were more reminiscent of quiet pilgrimages to Lourdes.

Actually Ursula's hospital room was ill suited to spiritual transfiguration. She was in the women's ward, section B, fifth floor, room 23. The whole of Westend Hospital smelled of doctor. You had to identify yourself elaborately at the reception desk, observe awkward visiting hours, and argue with obstinate nurses. The floors were polished to such a high shine that you could make your way through the long halls only by treading very carefully.

Ursula lay in a high, white-enameled bed, strangely wrapped and tied. A lot of apparatus surrounded her, and many brown hoses connected many glass ampuls to the bed. Apparently she was being artificially fed, and she must have been artificially emptied out as well. The whole mysterious area below her waist, which had always been considered low and dirty in our house, had been transformed into art, had become the pure art of the doctors, and under this subterfuge her face bloomed more attractive and beautiful than ever.

She lay like someone in a state of rapture; she could speak again a little. Softly, by fits and starts, words came from her scab-covered lips, and like all suicides who awaken into life once more, she repented of her deed. She displayed a silent determination to take it all back, and the doctors confirmed her hope—of course, certainly, she'd be home in three or four weeks, perhaps in a wheelchair; she's have to put up with the inconvenience for a while.

Thus Ursula went through a distinct phase of regeneration, and this period of vital recovery led my mother to the idea that was to deliver us. She had decided that Ursula must convert. That fateful Monday, she stated at dinner one day, had been a clear sign from above. Much was remiss in our family, much had already been criminally neglected at the time of her marriage. As a Catholic, she had wed without the blessings of her church, but Ursula's deathbed now gave her that forceful edge of moral superiority essential to the rectification of such early and grave errors.

Basically my father was indifferent to these

considerations. He was not interested in religion one way or another. It must have been his mother who, in the stiff-necked way of obdurate Protestants, had required the doctrinal humiliation of her daughter-in-law. But that had been long ago, on the day war broke out in 1914. His Protestant mother was dead, had been happily buried in the hill country of Brandenburg since 1931, and the Catholic tendency, long suppressed, suddenly became dominant in light of our affliction. Much was now to be revised.

Thus, on the afternoons when my mother was free of the hospital visits, she went in search of spiritual aid. The matter proved to be one of the utmost delicacy. On the one hand my mother insisted that help must come only from the better class of gentlemen, dignitaries of a higher rank, priests of the monastic orders, not profane, worldly clerics who led vulgar and questionable lives with their housekeepers and with many members of their Berlin congregations. On the other hand it was precisely these gentlemen of high theological standing who turned out to be the most obstinate. The cathedral prelates and monsignors to whom my mother had no trouble gaining access, the spiritual abbots and holy fathers, always quivered a little when, after quite a lot of respectable chatter, they heard mention of suicide. The situation was complicated, she was informed. The Church, the

Holy Mother, demanded of her children full spiritual clarity for such grave measures, and in fact physical wholeness was also needful. There was talk of total conversion, of complete repentance, and of grace. It became clear that it was precisely the gentlemen of the highest rank who were unwilling to serve as sanctified funeral directors. Thomas Aquinas had already argued ...

But in the meantime my mother had argued as well. In the early evening hours, when we used to leaf through the local paper, she had instead begun to peruse pious tomes and had found a sentence that she now enlisted in her cause. She had bought the *Confessions* of Saint Augustine in a pocket edition costing two marks and eighty pfennigs, and she spent long hours diligently studying it. Thus had she discovered the sentence that seemed to her suitable, like a key to the heart of the Church and her daughter. "Our heart is not quiet until it rests in Thee," the sentence read. "The poor child, our Ursi," she now liked to say. "Her unquiet heart. She was searching for God all the time."

The sentence really was suitable. I do not know to how many churches, chapels, monastic establishments, and clerical offices between Friedrichstrasse and Grunewald my mother hastened, but she displayed extraordinary energy and cunning in matters Catholic. One day she came home around six o'clock, quietly triumphant, acting gratified as she put her black handbag in our baroque wardrobe, turned the heavy key twice, pulled it out of the lock, locked this key in my father's desk, pulled out the key to the desk drawer as well, and declared as she locked the sideboard that everything was settled. Father Ambrose of the Salesians would be visiting the hospital the next day.

Father Ambrose was a short, amiable man with a bald head. He had a slight cast in one eye, but most of the time you didn't notice. He wore a black habit, had a cap on his bald pate, kept his eyes lowered, and came from somewhere in Zehlendorf; his motherhouse was in Freilassing near Salzburg. Actually he was not exalted enough for our case, and he seemed to be lacking in spiritual election as well. He displayed a unique kind of theological obstinacy and was intent on embarking upon a detailed course of lessons in conversion; he brought the catechism along and instructed the dying child from Eichkamp concerning the whence and whereto and why and wherefore of the world in general, enlightened her as to the intentions of the Creator, which were good and pure in themselves, and explained why, because of Eve, events had taken such an untoward turn.

This frightened my mother. "No formalities now," she sometimes said heatedly. "Just get on with it—the only thing that matters is the spirit."

She must have belonged to the left wing of Catholicism, and even in those days she rose up against the cold rationalism of the Thomist machinery of salvation. "Grace," she said. "All that matters is grace."

In fact there was danger in delay. Her daughter was still blossoming a little under the artificial feeding and emptying, but the rosiness and beauty of her face were already beginning to yield to the evil charm of death. And now that a spiritual mentor was assuming the reins, the doctors gradually stopped their ministrations in the sickroom and said sheepishly that the end might come any day now. Their skill was exhausted. "Another doctor must be called in," my mother exclaimed, and she did not mean Father Ambrose but Jesus. In those days we were afloat on a sea of piety.

On April 11, 1938—it was a Tuesday, ten o'clock in the morning—this other doctor arrived. Room 23 was transformed into a small, blooming chapel. The smell was no longer of doctor; the scent of Catholic was everywhere. Many flowers in the room, holy pictures on the walls, a small font of holy water by the door. A real altar with candles and crucifix was erected in one corner; and a bit of martyr's bone, the altar stone required by Roman custom, was brought by Father Ambrose in a black leather pouch that, like an overnight case, was fitted out very practically with an assortment of sacred utensils for every occasion. From it he took the holy implements needed for the administration of baptism, the subsequent confession, the subsequent mass complete with holy communion, and the subsequent extreme unction.

I was astonished and taken aback by so many rites. Four sacraments were being administered at one fell swoop, and if my mother had been allowed to choose a bishop, confirmation might have been added. There was no limit to grace; it poured over the sinner from Eichkamp like a torrent and washed her wonderfully clean. Through it all Father Ambrose exchanged verses of Scripture with an acolyte, donned different garments, drizzled water across Ursi's forehead, got a stole and some books ready, prayed interminably, and later mixed an oil. In between there was much incense, tinkling of a bell, and candlelight. Tears, too, were now in order—tears of sorrow and bliss.

For a while we were all sent out of the room. Probably it was time to hear confession, and I tried to imagine what she might be saying. How often she had pilfered and secretly snacked, how often she had been naughty and had impure thoughts? It was inconceivable. I stood at the corridor window staring fixedly at the traffic in the street. Down below, people walked as if nothing had happened: housewives and storm troopers, some with dogs. Charlottenburg went on living. My mother was holding a rosary and sobbing intermittently. It was hard to tell whether we were at a wedding or a funeral, but in fact it was a baptism, the celebration of our second birth—and, in our special case, also a celebration of our blessed grief. Father Ambrose, too, had mentioned *felix culpa*. Thus in the end everything turned to the good, and he had quoted a poet unknown to us: Each pain leaves us richer, praise consecrates misery.

She was dead. Yesterday she passed peacefully away. She could not defend herself against the evil poison or the pious ecstasy. Now she lay there, rigid, stiff, and white, and an odor of sanctity emanated from her. She had gone ahead of us all and would now ascend to heaven. Her eyes were shut in devotion, her mouth was closed, a rosary was wound around her folded hands like gentle shackles—shackles of love that no one could undo. The balm of faith had turned her into a bride of Christ, and yet she lay like a heavy bundle of silence, sealed and softly wrapped in twine.

This was how pharaohs' daughters lay on their biers, wood and paint, wax and bandages fashioning them into masks of eternity. They have shut you up, they have sealed you, they have stylized you with the bandages of faith. German opera in Charlottenburg—the church standing on the left, the populace to the right, both joining in with lively choruses—the celebration being called Death and Transfiguration, Gloria and Canonization of the Little Saint of Eichkamp.

Hold tight to these bindings, Ursula, or everything will fall apart. Inside you everything is broken; your body has turned to pulp, your kidneys are gruel and have flooded your heart with urine. Between your sex and your intestines is where it all began. Why won't you say it? Say it: It was never right, everything was terrible, awful, and life at our house was an everlasting torture. Why don't you say it? This soil was bad, worn out, putrid and decaying; the houses of Eichkamp could raise only poisonous toadstools of death.

There was so much fear in you, and you were always alone. Everything was so narrow, so rigid, so neatly strapped down. Later, when you grew older, you felt something like love inside you and did not know what to do with it. Repellent experience at seventeen: you were walled up, incarcerated in the prison of your body; you felt love and did not know what to do with it. There was no pole to attract it, no direction in which it could be drawn, no window through which you could see outside. There was no door in Eichkamp that could be pushed open. Everything was locked inside you. You drowned in your youth, choked, perished of your own energy. Perhaps you needed a husband and many children—that would have been a way out—but you could no longer get out of yourself. This world out here, this father, this mother—you did not want them, they did not want you. I do understand you, my sister!

It must be a deliverance to escape such prisons by death. It must have been hope you felt when you first saw the glass tube with the skull and crossbones. I can imagine it: a huge hope that now something would have to happen. That is how nothingness rises from the depths, making its way like damp through the walls of a generation, eating its way into the flesh of the children and suddenly erupting; it is called tragedy, but it became more of a family celebration, a mediocre comedy of love.

The day after Ursula's death my mother sat down at our small black-lacquered desk and announced to the public what had befallen us. She spoke on the telephone with newspapers and printing plants, took out neatly phrased advertisements, ordered many black-bordered postal announcements to carry our misfortune rapidly into the world. She arranged three requiem masses and summoned all our relatives to the celebration of the funeral. It was to be a ceremony of grace in spite of everything.

Together with Father Ambrose, my parents arrived at the realization that Ursula had entered on eternity in the venerable state of virginity. Even in those days there was much deploring of the fact that this state was becoming increasingly rare. Thus she was among the innocent children. She was *virgo intacta*, as my mother was able to establish with spiritual help. For a long time I could not understand why she was now introducing this peculiar phrase into every conversation. She told the neighbors and the doctors, she spread the word in the flower shop and assured the stonemason that he was dealing with that rare case, a genuine *intacta*. Apparently Ursula had never become soiled. The phrase rang strangely in my ears. I knew about con*tact* and *tact*ile, but now I heard the hard *a*'s like sharp blows of a hammer, and I had to look long and hard in the dictionary before I understood that we were talking about a different kind of touching.

In fact the advantages were impressive. Father Ambrose had called our attention to a time-honored tradition of the church: *virgines intactae* were as innocent children before God and therefore, like actual children, were entitled to a white burial. Now gladness and heavenly rejoicing were in order, and the business with the white coffin topped by a silver-ornamented virgin's wreath stirred us greatly and provoked deep thought. It was clearly demonstrated after all how worthwhile it was not to sleep with men. Ursula would sleep her way into eternal life blissfully, in white, almost like a nun. And the words of the poet were confirmed once more: Praise be to consecrated misery.

A few days later they all came, those we had summoned. They came with their hats thickly swathed in veiling, and in their fat suitcases they brought a great deal of Silesian sympathy. Uncle Hans and Aunt Anna came from Neuzelle. From their grocery store in Adolf Hitler Strasse they brought a scent of cinnamon and coziness to Berlin. Uncle Oswald came from Grünberg. He was called Sour Ossi because the tart Grünberg wine to which he was secretly addicted had lent him a cheerfully morose bachelor's expression. The more refined Flickschuhs came from Frankfurt on the Oder. They lived in perpetual discord with their vicar and sustained a considerable correspondence on the subject with the supervising bishopric. Hermann the teacher and Gertrude his wife came from Glatz. They had ten children at home. All of these mourners were Catholic, seemed warm and pudgy, set their suitcases down peremptorily in our narrow hall, looked in vain along the walls for the customary holy-water stoups, and fervently begged for a look at the young woman who had passed away before her time.

Then the Protestants came from the north. There was Aunt Alma from Stettin, an aging, spindly postal employee who spoke with a Saxon accent and had cleverly retired from her job as a telephone operator as early as 1930. Since that time she had lived alone with her cat on an unspeakably meager pension, had developed a spinster's miserliness to a high art, had added to it the pride of an old-time German state employee, and now constantly admonished us about living on much too lavish a scale. In those days she was collecting tinfoil and wastepaper for the army; without thrift, she said, no state could prosper. Then came Uncle Hans and Aunt Eva from Hamburg-Eidelstedt—Herr and Frau Lieutenant Commander, who still showed signs of adventures in the tropics. They had yellow, leathery skin, seemed very angular and hard, and were somewhat stuck-up in the Hanseatic manner. All day long they nervously reached for "ciggies," as Aunt Eva called their chain-smoking, and they infused our narrow rooms with an alien, pungent aroma of worldliness. They did not look for holy-water stoups, they asked for whiskey. Aunt Alma considered such requests sheer profligacy.

And both sides, wrapped in black Sunday finery, eyed each other suspiciously. They had known each other only by hearsay so far and immediately commenced lying in wait to see who would be the first to reveal a vulnerable spot. In spite of their numerical superiority, the Catholics clearly occupied the underdog position. They had an air of looseness and cunning. It must have been that they had too much heart and too little brain—as the Protestants, of whom the reverse was true, spitefully insinuated by sarcastic little turns of phrase.

Uncle Hans from Neuzelle and Uncle Hans from Hamburg, however, shared a common bond. Both were members of the Party, one out of loyalty, the other from conviction. They came to the funeral proudly wearing Party badges on their right lapels so that those of us who lived in the big city would not think that they were just anybody. It seemed to me at the time that on Uncle Hans the Catholic the swastika looked much more pleasant and familiar. On Uncle Hans the Protestant it was a different symbol; it seemed cold and foreign, coming from the north. Having spent the "era of the system," as he put it, on Java, he was once again an officer, teaching in a U-boat school.

And all of them thronged our little house, which was suddenly full of life and activity. They asked for sheets, blankets, and chamber pots, they wanted to read the newspapers and listen to the radio, they talked now and then about the return of Austria and said that at last the dreams of the Führer's youth in Vienna had come true. Between times wreaths were delivered and flower arrangements with large bows arrived; all the pine greenery made it smell like Christmas. At intervals my mother retired to the den to receive callers paying their condolences. Aunt Alma slept in Ursula's bed, and I had to move into the kitchen because the more refined Flickschuhs, who corresponded with the bishopric, were to spend the night in my room.

The gathering turned into a long and unforgettable family celebration that reached its climax, as is usual in such cases, only after the funeral. It was the custom to go out for the funeral repast, but my mother, together with Aunt Alma, had prepared the feast at home. It was consonant with family spirit in such an hour of greatness not to rent an unfamiliar and purely commercial place in the city.

We had always lived alone and quietly in Eichkamp. In the past my mother had managed to avert any announced visits from relatives with a hurried telegram regretfully declaring her illness at the time. Thus no one had come to see us for many years. We had lived as if we were in a beleaguered city, in a closed society, and we had remained entirely among ourselves.

That way of life had now come to an end. The fortress had been breached, the gate stood open, and Ursula's deathbed family rushed in from every direction, spreading through the halls, sitting in all the rooms, coming to rest in the kitchen, clambering up the stairs, stepping out into the garden, standing outside the front door. Relations oozed from every crack, creating a tense atmosphere. In those days I became acquainted with the joy of love for one's fellows, the comforting power of the extended family, from which, alas, we seem to be distancing ourselves.

In the late afternoon, around five o'clock, the celebration reached its apex. Our dining table had been opened to furnish a small festal board that by now was succumbing to a wild and at the same time pleasurable disintegration. Wineglasses and coffee cups stood about in total disarray. Never before had anything so brilliant, so festive, so wasteful, taken place in our dining room.

The elegant crystal goblets and the Meissen china, the asparagus dishes and the silver platters, which for tens of years had stiffly decorated our sideboard—artful displays subject to constant dusting—were now spread out recklessly. The death of the daughter brought them to life. In the kitchen precious silver knives and forks were awakened from decades of red-upholstered sleep in chests covered in black leather. It became evident at this juncture that we were people of considerable affluence. My parents' wedding presents were put to use for the first time in twenty-four years: napkin rings of heavy silver, engraved with the date 1914 in old-fashioned flourishes; ladles I had never seen before, their inner surfaces gilded, their handles monogrammed; and many dessert plates of heavy crystal that my mother released from long-locked cabinets.

Uncle Hans the Catholic was in a melancholy Burgundy mood. His sorrow was muffled, his mourning transfigured; as always after a good dinner, quiet contentment set in. An additional circumstance was that Father Ambrose sat directly across from him, having been unable to resist my mother's pleas to stop in for at least a moment. So now the devout Salesian sat within our four walls like a small spiritual showpiece, sat humbly at my mother's side as she had always dreamed. They sat together cheek by jowl, like Francis and Clara in Assisi, and surely everything would have gone off splendidly if Uncle Hans had not abruptly risen to his feet.

He stood up clumsily, with a snort, momentarily revealing a heavy gold chain across his stomach, three stag's teeth dangling from it. His face was red and shiny with ceremonial perspiration. He wiped it with his crumpled napkin, tapped his glass, put his cigar aside, and raised the goblet in his right hand. "Your excellency," I heard him say in a deep, gurgling voice, "Let us recall our dear departed one, who is now in heaven—with your help." Then he put down his glass, groped in his trouser pocket, and pulled out a brown, shiny wallet. Leafing through it, he withdrew a bill: fifty fat marks, which for a second he displayed both intimately and triumphantly to the group. Then he humbly placed the bill on Father Ambrose's cake plate, put a cake fork over it, and said, "Your excellency, a requiem mass for Ursula."

Father Ambrose may have wanted to wave it aside modestly, but he never had the chance, for something suddenly happened to me. I must have silently collapsed, for my head smacked sharply against a crystal dessert plate. The plate bounced aside with a bright clatter and danced merrily on our wooden floor. My insides were gripped by an agonizing spasm; starting at my stomach, everything was contracting, choking and pressing upward. My body lurched forward, and I must have lost consciousness for a second. When I came to again, I saw that I had vomited right across the table. Rust-colored slime spread over the white linen, reminding me immediately of Ursula's blood on the pillow. The brownish stuff gradually seeped through the cloth, forming circles, and when I felt its sour taste in my mouth, I was frightened and thought: Blood, only blood can leave such a taste in your mouth. I pulled myself upright, overturned my chair, and blindly ran out of the dining room, out of the kitchen. I ran into the garden and came to a stop somewhere near a wooden bench.

The calm of a springtime evening lay over the world. There was the smell of new grass, and blue pansies stood in full bloom. In the neighbors' garden someone was watering beds of fresh lettuce; sparrows were gliding across the wide blue sky, and somewhere a bicyclist was ringing his bell, making a bright and cheerful clang. A peaceful evening in Eichkamp.

Then I saw the kitchen door opening. My mother stepped out followed by Uncle Hans the Catholic, her brother. She was leaning on him. Both were veiled in black, and both came ever closer to me. I could not avoid them now, I could not flee, I could not take anything back. I felt the taste of blood in my mouth. Here came the family, my family. They would kill me. They had seen me, they were coming closer still. I heard my mother say to her brother, "But, Hans, she was his sister, after all." And I thought, Yes, that's right; of course, she was my sister.

At this I felt something bursting inside me, breaking, falling to pieces: my pride, my arrogance, my coldness. For the first time in three weeks the evil, awful rigidity left me. For the first time I was filled with pain—genuine, simple pain. Everything was suddenly fluid and shapeless. A feeling of vertigo overcame me. There was an abyss. I fell and fell and fell even deeper, I fell through all the shafts of the past—in a moment I would crash. I was a child again, and I wanted to cry again like a child, I wanted to bawl like a child. I wanted to be unhappy like a child. I wanted to be like every other child.

My Friend Vanya

Prague, they say, is a beautiful city. They say: To this day Prague is a beautiful city, especially today and again today, when some things are beginning to change. Golden, eternal Prague, baroque and Catholic, monumental and charming, the city on the Moldau, the crown of art. Go to Prague—it is still a magical city. The word *magical* should have made me suspicious.

Do you know Prague? What happened to me in Prague is what always happens to me in strange cities where I suddenly find myself after years of knowing them only by hearsay: at the beginning there is only disappointment. You arrive in the afternoon, always a Sunday afternoon, and on Sunday afternoons every city in the world is hell for strangers. You simply cannot get in, it is raining to boot, and everything vegetates so ceremoniously. Of course you've brought quite a bit of expectation with you: golden Prague, baroque and Catholic and still magical. In those days I failed at everything. You walk through the streets, empty and wet with rain. You go to Wenceslaus Square and look everywhere for the palace, the castle, and the Cathedral of Saint Vitus; you cross many damp bridges over the Moldau, saints and angels on each side, as marbly cold as in a thousand churches.

Prague is rich in palaces and noble mansions, true, but at the time that meant nothing to me. The only thing that mattered was that all of it conspired against me; the windows were shuttered, the gates kept their contents firmly locked away from me. The city was very empty and swept terribly clean of work, of life and trade. It looked as handsome and boring as someone's best parlor—a drawing room with lace cloths and many knickknacks. That was my Prague: the sense of walls, of stone, of vast emptiness, the taste of meaninglessness and disappointment. It was a pretty crazy and sick feeling.

Do you know the fragile and insidious temptation to cultivate this condition of disillusion to the point of loathing? Of course we have long since become prisoners of our own abysses. The road outward is blocked. Of course we always have a couple of addresses in our pockets, two or three telephone numbers; people like us won't go traveling any other way. Now would be the time to call. We do not call. We are already so enamored of the disappointment and the enjoyment of it.

We harbor malicious hopes of building up to a

great scene: to pack our bags in the morning and depart. I was there, but you'll never know. I was there, but I couldn't get in, for in actuality I wasn't there at all. I only walked along the streets and squares, the bridges and steps of Prague, and then I left. I was afraid—afraid of beginning, afraid of telephoning, afraid of saying, Here I am, I am here.

I could no longer do it in those days in Prague. I was deeply enmeshed in my fear and loneliness. I came from the West and brought with me a great deal of understanding for decay and decadence.

For such cases there is only one solution any-where in the world: Roma Termini, Gare du Nord, Grand Central. All the railroad stations in the world are dammed up with expectation, disap-pointment, and shattered happiness. We can con-nect with such feelings. Between colorful news-stands and dusty platforms life goes on; we can pick it up and find our way back. Railroad stations have tracks, timetables, and set fares—reliable things, facts we can cling to. In particular there are all the others who come to the train station because they are having the same experience. Every railroad waiting room is an assembly of the derailed, of those who have been thrown off the tracks, a meeting place of the homeless and the crazy. There is a smell of expectation and hope; all lonely people run around like animals and sniff each other like animals, signaling that the world outside contains the thing that in fact is only within: being lost. It is a pretty dreadful smell.

In Prague my salvation was a newsstand. Prague has far fewer newspapers and magazines than we have at home, and those there are look clearly paler and plainer. In Prague glossy depravity does not spring from the page, enticing the viewer into sinfulness. Nevertheless, there are newspapers there, and I bought one because I told myself, Maybe later sometime you'll be able to telephone. I bought *Neues Deutschland*, the official newspaper of East Germany. This was not a publication I had a great hankering for. It is simply too didactic and brisk and reminded me too much of the *Osservatore Romano* or a provincial diocesan newsletter; everything was so dry and ordered from above. But when you're in Prague and don't understand the language of the city and it is raining gently on a Sunday afternoon and you feel so silly, you're willing to take even that and say to yourself, The others, those in the East, have to read it every day; it can't hurt you this once.

No, I am not going to tell you how I finally managed after all to enter the city, to conquer it and find it as attractive as all the guidebooks proclaim. I will only say that on this abominably failed Sunday night I was in bed by eight thirty and that it happened there. The visitors' beds of socialism aren't bad at all. Of course, everything is a little old-fashioned and cumbersome, but doesn't that confer a certain security? It is like visiting an aristocratic grandmother in the country—everything very proper and in keeping with decent middle-class culture; still real hand-spun linen, none of that neo-German junk with convertible sofa bed and plastic shower such as they have in Düsseldorf or Frankfurt, where we get our neuroses from.

I had lit a cigar and was gulping down the remainder of some Western whiskey from a small pocket flask. I was a journalist from the West who had come to socialist Prague in April 1963 with his peculiarities, his arrogance, his cigars and whiskey flask, and his most recent neuroses, in order to find everything good and progressive. So what?

Even then *Neues Deutschland* was covering the brilliant successes of socialism in the Near East, especially in Egypt, where the Americans had just committed another of their indescribable follies. Even *Neues Deutschland* was incensed by this, and they featured it on the front page, under fat headlines. I read the opening line, which stated, "As our Near Eastern correspondent, Lothar Killmer, reports from Cairo..." Such banal and formulaic phrases open newspaper stories all over the world. Reports from agencies, reports from correspondents, Reuters and UPI and Tass—one skims the words blindly, as one should, and I did too for a few seconds; no longer. The name had reached me.

Sometimes a name has an inexplicable impact. Scientists probably call this phenomenon threshold stimulation or release effect. I saw only the name—not at all an unusual one—read it over and over, and suddenly I knew: he was there once, there was someone like that in my life. Of course—that's what it must be. That is how one falls back, sliding through the shafts of time as in an elevator, rushing downward to where there is only childhood, thick and sentimental and pulpy. And so I knew abruptly, with a wordlesss sensation of childish emotion—of course, it must be Vanya. Finally I'd been given a sign of him—after twenty years.

Senior Assistant Master Focken was a man of the old school, a Prussian man of learning. A trace of humanistic helplessness and Protestant inwardness clung to him when, with a shamefaced "Heil Hitler," he entered the classroom. He tried to get the formalities out of the way quickly. He wore puttees and tight-fitting green forest rangers' suits with high patch pockets. This gave him, a man already in his late fifties, an air both decently German and hoary. The skinniness of his legs and the narrowness of his Protestant male chest were quite evident in such fashionable garments.

Herr Focken taught us classical languages; he taught us the strange sayings, the well-modulated prattle of a German middle-class education—the stuff we call our inalienable heritage. From Xenophon to Erasmus, from Tacitus to Luther, from the Protestant hymnal to the Brothers Grimm, he found it all deep and serious and worth taking to heart, and he did in fact urge it upon us in all sincerity.

Singing was another thing he liked to do. Even as late as 1936 he opened our Latin lesson by delivering in a high, bold voice, "Lord, Thy Goodness Is Everlasting," singing alone and confidently, clasping his hands across his body firmly, yet with the fingers splayed a little. His right eye, blue, turned a little outward, so that one did not know where he was looking as he sang.

Herr Focken's relations to the new state were formulated in the one phrase that in Germany had already sent whole generations happily to their graves: *mens sana in corpore sano.* Herr Focken was equally ardent about Plato, Luther, and Walter Flex, the "ideal German boy." Herr Focken had volunteered in the First World War—cheerful and God-fearing, as he said—and the course of his service had strongly reinforced his attitude of German inwardness. "Fellows," he sometimes said, distorting his lips into a grimace òf wild pedagogical determination that secretly made us boys giggle, "fellows, remember Walter Flex: a sound mind can live only in a sound body." And yet it seemed that all his limbs were creaking. Resolutely he pulled himself upright.

One day Herr Focken did not arrive alone. How could I ever forget? Berlin, the autumn of 1936, shortly after the Olympic Games, in the second half of the fifth form of the Grunewald Gymnasium, which today is called Walter Rathenau School because it is just around the corner from Königsallee, where Walter Rathenau was shot—but in those days we didn't know a thing about that. Herr Focken showed up with a pile of black notebooks, his songbook, and Vanya, a boy who looked a little like those pictures of wild children raised by wolves.

It was an indescribably comical scene: the two of them suddenly appeared in the doorway and were about to say "Heil Hitler," but at that moment the notebooks slipped from Herr Focken's arms. Twenty-nine black notebooks clattered to the floor, and the new boy plunged on top of them quick as a flash to remedy the mishap. Both his arms roiled through the pile, swept the books together, and promptly let them fall again, accomplishing all this with an air of breathless assistance that at the same time seemed to parody its own fruitlessness. Diabolos, the rogue and poltergeist, had arrived.

"A new boy," Herr Focken said, threading his way elegantly over the black heap on his skinny legs. He opened his songbook and commenced, looking resolutely upward. He was also singing for Lothar Killmer.

The new boy was short, stocky, and tanned. He had a husky body and short, brawny arms and legs. His hair hung messily into his face, and it was scruffy at the back of his neck, where he had a large birthmark. Thoroughly unkempt, he seemed to have come from a different world. For our school he was exceedingly coarse. In those days most of my classmates were refined and neat, coming from a better class of people, sons of the Prussian bourgeoisie, smooth and with a superficial trace of lordliness even at sixteen. They were sons of manufacturers, of regional court judges, and of officers. Someday, like their fathers, they would ride for an hour every morning or play tennis or meet after work for convivial nights out.

In those days Grunewald was extremely high-toned: estates at the edge of the water, with large gardens; old mansions, Protestant, Prussian, and somewhat aristocratic. These were surely the twilight days of the class that perished on July 20, 1944. They were the elite, as they say in our neck of the woods, and I did not fit in. It didn't take me long to figure it out. The new boy and I belonged together. One day I realized that we were meant for each other. He had not been among us for more than three or four weeks, and he had been sharing my desk for quite awhile. After I had prompted him vigorously on a boring Xenophon translation, he slipped me a note. It read, "My name is Vanya, don't tell anybody." It was then I sensed that he would be the dearest friend of my youth.

Does anyone know what friendship is exactly? What is it? Two things mesh, two things form a unit, two things bond, though they always seem separate on the outside. In the other person we look for ourselves, for the possibilities we do not act out. Vanya was my other chance, the life I never would have had the strength to lead. In those days he opposed the prevailing order in a most outrageous manner. It took me a long time to realize this fact, and it attracted me.

Vanya was completely different, and he had just about every failing it was possible to have in Berlin-Grunewald during the Hitler years. He came from a proletarian family, he was half Jewish and half Russian, and his mother, as the von Kleists and von Mansteins whispered amid giggles during recess, was a working person, a "miss," a Miss Worker from Halensee. For awhile it was said that he was the illegitimate son of Litvinov, the Russian foreign minister. This was a romantic rumor, though the truth never became clear between us; he refused to tell me anything at all about his father. For reasons I never understood, his father was Vanya's Achilles' heel.

Vanya was the personification of the outsider. He was not at home anywhere, and yet he had used his fate to forge a wonderful position of independence. He was absolutely free, and he took fierce pleasure in the joys of freedom. He enjoyed being alive, enjoyed taking part, enjoyed grasping the world. He was healthy, strong, and of a splendid simplicity—all doubts and questions dissolved in his grin, in the way he made a face. He loved life. He went swimming and boating, he boxed, and by the time he was seventeen, he had a girl friend with whom he slept on the weekends.

On Monday mornings we met at seven-thirty at Halensee Station. He always arrived a little late, sleepy and a little rumpled, and as we set out on our way to school, he told me of the various pleasures of premature wedded bliss, what he liked about women and what he could do without. There was authority in his disquisitions. Even as we were going up the steps to the school building, he would change the subject, perhaps reporting on a secret conspiracy between Trotsky and Hitler. All this was very foreign to me. I walked silently at his side and listened to the dusky sounds of his voice, fearful of Latin class and fearful of Greek. We were eighteen years old.

Vanya was my adventure, and I became deeply involved in it. He possessed so much life, life that I could not achieve. He was simply there, completely there. Nothing in the world could deflect him from his determination to find life good. He was really quite ugly, but the force of his presence only made him more virile. He was not smart, and his education was basically deficient, but he knew what was important at a particular moment, and in ticklish situations he confronted our teachers, whom he despised, with surprising and audacious counterquestions that threw them into confusion.

"All right," he said to me sometimes, "so you're pretty smart. But you haven't got what it takes."

"What it takes?" I asked. "What is that?"

"Desire," he answered.

And again I asked, "Desire for what?"

"For madness," he replied.

"For madness?"

"Yes," he insisted. "You need some mad desire to be here."

Of course I became his slave. Slowly and inevitably I fell under his spell. You have to be eighteen to fall so helplessly under someone else's sway. When you're older, you don't give yourself away anymore. Every time I went to see him, I handed myself over. It was always a journey into another world; I was entirely filled with astonishment.

Vanya lived behind Halensee Station in a shabby and dark tenement building. Never before had I found myself in such streets. The odor of poverty and old age was everywhere—heavy, creaking doors; worn-down steps; cabbage fumes throughout the house. I had to climb up four flights, and then I stood before an old-fashioned opaque glass door, its jamb studded with many calling cards affixed with thumbtacks. An aging man let me in grumpily and eyed me suspiciously. In the hallway threadbare carpets hung at the doors to the rooms. Musical instruments and tobacco pipes lined the soiled walls. Smells came from the kitchen, a woman's voice was singing, and then Vanya stepped out from behind one of the ragged carpets.

He was disguised in a highly romantic way. He sported a red Russian tunic with a rakish neckerchief, he wore short green trousers, and his bare feet were stuck into felt slippers. He said, "Come on, come in here." His voice was inviting and unfamiliar, as if that very morning we had not shared a schoolbench. He was a different person here, alien and mysterious, and he led me into a realm that was foreign to me, that enticed and scared me.

Yes, he was completely different. His room

was like an opium den of the poor—everything made of boards, crates, sleazy fabrics, pillows, rug scraps. Many dog-eared books were scattered over the floor. There was no table, no chair; everything was on the floor. A world for crouching, for lying, for sleeping. Under the window something resembling a bed had been set up: a mattress with a lot of pillows and disarranged blankets rested on the bare wood. A samovar bubbled in a corner.

Vanya's world was a ludicrous mixture of Russian anarchism and old-Berlin proletariat. In the midst of the Hitler years he and his mother continued to live in the wild, romantic-proletarian style of the Roaring Twenties. His room was a stage for a private social revolution. I would never have believed that such a thing existed in Germany. I would never have thought it possible that something of the sort could stand shoulder to shoulder with Eichkamp. Where we lived, everything was good and decent, bright and elevated, and of a repulsive mediocrity. Everything rigid and stiff and empty, one house like another, an arid bureaucracy of existence. Here, at Vanya's house, there was savagery, chaos, a gulf of enigmas and inconceivabilities—surely I had no choice but to fall under the spell of this gulf.

I went to Vanya's house more and more frequently. I went secretly and with a bad conscience and was more and more mesmerized by him, by the unabashed poverty that promised such an unexplored wealth of life. Vanya made tea, all the time lecturing me on the culture of tea. He brought out an old, shredded paperback book and began to read: *Okakura Kakuzo—The Book of Tea*. And later he fetched one of the musical instruments from the hall. It was a balalaika, he explained; I had never heard the word before. Then he sang songs I had never heard before either, with words I did not understand—Russian folk songs. They were dark and melancholy, wild and occasionally plangent with a tenderness he could never quite capture. Now Vanya was at a great distance from me. He was a horseman, a cossack, a lord, a peasant boy singing of a faraway home; he was a poet singing of remote revolutions, of civil wars, of flight and hunger and love. He plucked the strings and softly translated some of the lines: "Parasha, when you grow to love me, I will feel like a general—yes, like a general." And soon he began to laugh, pushed everything sloppily to one side, and rolled and lit a cigarette. The way his short, plump fingers first bent the little cardboard tube showed me his total mastery. In his poverty he was king.

Of course my parents watched this friendship with growing displeasure. They were dismayed to see their son, who one day might be a priest, or at least a civil servant in the Prussian state, in such degenerate company. In their view the relationship was a bad one. Vanya was strange to them, and sinister. We were nineteen by now, about to take our final examinations. He had grown a little taller and even stockier, had a trace of unruly moustache about his lips, and was still unkempt and furry of nape. We were in my room, which was pale and insipid and colorless. I was reading to him from Nietzsche and Hölderlin, trying with the helpless postures of idealism to reveal to him my own exalted middle-class world. I spoke of Zarathustra and supermen and of the fact that all of us must develop beyond ourselves toward a distant and final goal. Rilke, too, was mentioned.

Vanya sat on the floor—he did not like chairs. He was smoking some cheap weed in a homemade pipe and staring silently into the distance. He wore a blue Russian tunic and coarse brown trousers tucked into roughly fashioned sheepskin boots. All he did was smoke and keep his silence, sometimes spitting absently, and it was his spitting that abruptly revealed my hopelessness to me. Everything was so pointless and empty. What was I saying? My words were futile. I dropped *Hyperion* and *Zarathustra*. I walked to the window, and I heard Vanya begin to hum a song. His voice was deep and his tone melancholy: "...yes, like a general."

I felt a dark misery, a terrible rage in myself. I looked down on the streets of Eichkamp: dead ends all of them, all of them errors, all of them wrong turnings, even if they were dolled up with Hölderlin and Nietzsche. Eichkamp streets all led to nothingness; there was no life here. Suddenly I began to hate Vanya. I hated him, he made me feel so small and powerless, he was so much my superior. I ran away, fled down the stairs. My mother was standing at the stove stirring a Silesian soup, and she said, "Do you have to keep bringing him here? They do say that he's half Jewish. My God, son, you'll bring misfortune on us all."

The misfortune had a bright and mysterious beginning, and actually it was Vanya's misfortune—it touched me only tangentially. We were now twenty years old. We had long since survived Herr Focken and Walter Flex, and we were done with school. Life, for which they prepared us so thoroughly and for so long, was beginning. At the time my fortunes were rising rapidly. Like all Germans, I was aiming high. I began to study philosophy, I was reading Kant and Hölderlin and Nietzsche, and at night I paid secret visits to Vanya, whom I hated and loved and could not leave. We do not learn for school but for life.

Since our graduation Vanya had changed. He had become more serious, more secretive. A trace of taciturnity marked his features, and when on a particular evening—it was April 1939—I rang his doorbell, I suddenly realized: the time of childhood is over.

It was quiet in his apartment. Candles burned, and as before, everything was scattered on the floor in a romantic way. But a woman was present; in the semidarkness she was squatting on the mattress, and it was a while before the cigarette smoke floating slowly upward made me aware that she was there. Vanya said, "That's Anni Korn." And to her he said, "That's him, Mush. Look him over."

Later there was a long supper prepared mysteriously by Anni Korn behind the exotic hangings in the hall. It was an outlandish and pungent dish that burned on my tongue for a long time. Couscous or something like that, with a lot of garlic and pepper, served with vodka and Russian cigarettes. Afterward Anni Korn read aloud—something by Gorky. She was blond and slender, with a sharp expression etched between her nose and her lips, and she seemed much older than we were. Surely she must have been past thirty. In her presence Vanya was quieter and not so self-assured. Somehow she exerted a power over him that I could not define. I could see that there was a bond between them, though I did not yet understand it; it was a bond of quiet, silent intimacy, implicit in all their movements. It excluded me, simply left me out. I was filled with disappointment and something like jealousy.

Finally, past midnight, she abruptly put down

102

her book, pulled a briefcase from behind the pillow, and squatted tailor-fashion on the mattress. Lighting another cigarette, she gave me a sharp look, inhaled the smoke deeply, let it come out of her mouth again in sporadic, sharp bursts. She spoke into the darkness. "Is it true that you'll be working with us? You are one of us, aren't you?"

And I did not understand. I had no idea what she was talking about or what she was doing there. I looked helplessly at Vanya and heard him say, "Of course you'll be working for us. Just please don't ask a lot of questions."

That was how, in the spring of 1939—the Protectorate of Bohemia and Moravia had just joined the Reich—I found myself a member of an illegal group working against Hitler in the heart of Germany, in the heart of the Third Reich. I was utterly astonished. I had never sought it out, never asked for it. I was never a hero; I just fell into it. I hated this state, but it would never have occurred to me that it was possible to oppose it. Whatever came from the top was precisely that: the word from the top. It was fate, providence, or grace, in any case always predestined, as Herr Focken told us when talking about the heroes of Greece. I would never have thought that action could be taken against Hitler; I would never have believed that he was not fated. He was as great as the Greek gods, and far more powerful.

But I did take the letters Anni Korn pulled out

of the briefcase, twelve or thirteen of them, fully sealed and tied. The envelopes were pale yellow and bore no addresses. They had small numbers where one usually put the stamps. I took the list she gave me, and in the next few days I delivered the letters according to the list and carefully erased the numbers and saw so many houses. Berlin is as big and wide as the world and has as many front doors as the world. You could spend your life delivering letters there.

It must have been some kind of courier service they picked me for. Later the business with the flyers started, which quickly broke all our backs. One fine day we were all arrested.

It was two years before I saw Vanya again. That was outside the People's Courthouse in Berlin, where for many years, on many floors, many trials against traitors were conducted. Ours was on the third floor.

The war had long since started; Poland, Holland, Belgium, and France had long since been conquered. It was the spring of 1941, and our country was in the throes of a final frenzy of victory and enthusiasm. Germany was like an addict who would soon collapse, who would soon be no more than a little clump of misery, but now she had shot up one more time, once more felt the raging fever of power. There had been so many lightning campaigns—orgasms of war. The Germans were almost drunk with their good fortune. They said that the time had come to invade England, and they already had a song for the crossing; everyone said that at last we would move against England, and no one thought of Russia, with whom we were allied. All Germany was filled with flags, with uniformed heroes who, as the saying goes, were covered with glory. The war was an enormous victory celebration marching across Europe. Germany lay over the continent like a war cloud and was busy building the new Europe of Germanic splendor.

The court was another theater of war: war on the home front, war against the traitors, the spies and saboteurs. As I entered the large hearing room on the third floor, blood-red colors blew in my direction—flags, pennants, uniforms. I too was in uniform, in the outfit of our paratroopers. I was a German soldier who had come from France, summoned as a witness against Vanya. They had ordered me to report here straight from Caen.

Vanya, how can I ever forget this moment? Where were you? I could not find you. I saw only the crimson flags and the sea of uniforms in the auditorium. At the front, against the wall behind the judges' bench, a huge banner was unfurled; it must have been fifteen or twenty meters long. On it was a soaring silver eagle, small and sharp.

Under it sat twelve men at a long table that was also covered by a red cloth; three of the men were in civilian clothing. These twelve were the judges, I was told, and the three were lawyers, which is to say that the other nine were representatives of the people, who had to do the judging.

Along the right and left sides of the hall rows of seats had been erected, as in a theater. They were filled by Party members and army officers, the gentlemen of the central leadership, who had to attend such trials daily in order to familiarize themselves from the outset with the techniques and tricks of the enemy. They would protect the people against the people's enemies. A play was to be performed for them. The play began in the apartment behind Halensee Station. It was called *Vanya and His Friend*, or *Lothar Killmer and Anni Korn*. There was an icy atmosphere here: a national theater of power, where everyone was silent and lowered his head and stared rigidly into space and only one person shouted. Here this was called a trial.

And finally I discovered him. Small and pale and hunched over, he sat on a bench to one side; the woman next to him must have been Anni Korn. After two years' imprisonment they were barely recognizable, so small and white and silent had they become. Their heads were shrunken, and from a distance they stood out against the colorful background like white mice. Lots of green-clad men stood close behind them. Vanya and Anni were chained to each other, and both together were chained to some of the green ones.

They had put my childhood in irons, they had put handcuffs on the foolish dream of my youth. Something was converging, something was being linked—something that would always remain separate on the outside. There sat my Diabolos, there sat my piece of madness, no longer stirring. They had captured him, and I stood on the side of the free, the victors. I was one of them, I wore their uniform and their national emblem; I had always been so timid and clever and careful, and now I felt wretched.

My God, I always lacked your strength and your madness, Vanya. You said no, and I said yes. It had become an insane world: yes or no, now we were all caught in the web. Some killed, and the others were killed; some judged, and the others were judged. It had become a confused and horrifying world, all of us trapped. The world was divided into two camps: there were only the persecutors and the persecuted. Yes or no, we were all caught.

How to go on telling this story? Where do I begin? Stories written by life are hard to tell. They are so direct. Probably I should talk now about the return from Prague, how I came back to Frankfurt with nothing but the name of Lothar Killmer on my mind. It was a guess and more, and it gave me no peace. I thought: A name, that doesn't mean anything, a name read in a newspaper in Prague after twenty years; there are so many names in this world. And then again I thought: Maybe. It could be him, it could just be a lucky coincidence. Who knows these things in this crazy world?

The name gave me no peace. So one day I wrote to *Neues Deutschland* asking whether their Near Eastern correspondent from Cairo was one and the same Lothar Killmer. It was just possible, if you think of the games life plays. After four or five weeks I actually received a reply from East Berlin. On gray, official paper *Neues Deutschland* informed me that it *was* him, it was indeed him if my facts were correct; they would check them out. Later—after they had checked—they wrote that they could unfortunately not give me his address in Cairo, for their correspondents always traveled a great deal, but I could write directly to *Neues Deutschland* or, better still, come to their offices; old antifascists were always welcome in their organization.

Then there were endless negotiations, stretching over more than six months. My story had been clarified in the meantime, and Vanya had also vouched for me with his newspaper. After a considerable hiatus they wrote just before Christmas suggesting that I come at once, for he would also be arriving. In fact *Neues Deutschland* always organized a big journalists' convocation between Christmas Eve and New Year's. At that time the people's correspondents were introduced to the people, and they had to account for themselves in Dresden and Weimar and Rostock. That's socialism's idea of a holiday, a present from *Neues Deutschland* to the people and to its correspondents. It was to be bestowed on me as well.

So I met with Vanya. It was Christmas 1964. It was a stirring and painful reunion—I should never have done it. We cannot catch up with our dreams. We did not meet in the offices of *Neues Deutschland*; they were simply too efficient and official for the holidays. We met in the Press Café at Friedrichstrasse Station, which is frequented by all the visitors from the West who believe they owe such a visit to their intellectual standing. It is a kind of gathering point for the intelligentsia, or the cultural workers, as they say there—I never quite mastered the language of progressivism.

For a while I sat alone at the little table, which reminded me of the famous Café Kranzler during the 1930s. The tables there were all heavy glass and stiff as ramrods, like everything in the cozy Prussia of the 1930s; even the menu under glass, with a long handle and heavily silvered on the underside, promised old pleasures at 1930 prices. Everything was very proper.

I had ordered tea with lemon. They said there was no lemon for tea, and they said it as if I had asked for something indecent. Later a woman sat down at my table, an old lady with the face of a North German grandmother who had seen better days. The old lady began to drink coffee, making lots of refined motions; she apparently had also requested something indecent, because she was told that there was no cream, that the condensed milk of the German Democratic Republic was sufficient. Granted, these are trivialities, and a person who has gone through the business with Vanya and Hitler and the People's Tribunal shouldn't waste words on them. I was only grieved by the tone in which they said what they said. In the "New Germany" of the East they always felt provoked, and they had a pointed and categorical style of rebuke that intended to base itself on Karl Marx but that reminded me only of dissatisfied women: nursing nuns in hospitals, or English governesses. They kept on instructing and chastising us. I did not care for it.

After a while the old lady, who must have been able to tell by looking at me that I came from the West, struck up a conversation. Her eyes searched my features. Of course the conversation began with cream and moved on to condensed milk and from there to sugar, real objects about which old ladies know more than we do. She praised the sugar because it came from Cuba, but surely our sugar was better, she said; everything that was ours was better. She looked at me testingly, suspiciously, expectantly, and she was genuinely disappointed when I disagreed. Not everything that was ours was better, I said; that was no way to look at it.

Then she gradually started telling stories, slipped into her own memories, long-submerged experiences she'd brought along from a village near Rostock. She talked of storing potatoes for the winter and complained about how *they* had brought her family's three hundred pounds back up out of the cellar although the lot had been officially apportioned to them and had been doing very nicely there in the dark; and in general, about the way *they* pushed everyone around—for meat coupons, herring, and twenty-five grams of butter a day. Oh well, she interrupted after a pause, as if to reassure herself, Berlin—you had to admit it was a paradise on earth.

As the woman started in again and was coming to life because she had found someone who would listen to all her stories as if they were strange tales from a foreign land and would only shake his head now and then—that was when Vanya arrived. I recognized him at once by his

111

stocky body and the birthmark on his neck, and I was shocked. Suddenly I was afraid of the madness of reunion. For a second I thought, No, anything but that, it's wrong, it cannot happen. It simply cannot happen that we act as if there were only twenty-three years between us—there are centuries between us. How can you bridge centuries?

But there was no way to stop now; he must have recognized me too. Vanya was always so assured. He made straight for me. The woman at my table opened her mouth in astonishment and looked at us, a little fearful and perplexed. I had risen to my feet, and now both of us stood there shaking hands like old buddies, laughing and trying for a somewhat helpless, awkward embrace and the kind of kiss that characterizes socialist state visits. These are the tried and true gestures of reunion, the body's sign language, intended to help us over the seconds of speechlessness.

How to begin, what to say, and what is most important now? What should be most important after twenty-three years? More often than not we do it wrong; we get tangled up in some triviality, we say something totally banal, we talk about the checkroom ticket, about the weather, or about the terrible service. Nothing but being at a loss, nothing but subterfuge. Best to begin at once with the physical aspects and say, "You've hardly changed, Vanya," thinking all the time, *Actually he used to look different.* I said, "I recognized you the minute you came in the door, Vanya," thinking, *What is it about him? He looks so decent and settled. The mystery has left him.* I said, "You've come a long way, Vanya," thinking, *What is it about him? His madness is gone. Now he wears an insipid gray business suit, his hair is neatly parted, and the nape of his neck is clean.*

Like anyone else, Vanya sat in chairs now. He looked just like anyone else except that on his jacket he wore a lot of insignia, silver, red, and speckled badges that meant nothing to me. "How are you doing these days?" I finally asked in distress. It was a pretty offensive question after twenty-three years of Hitler and Ulbricht, and it could elicit only an equally offensive answer. Vanya said, "Very well, my dear chap. We are all doing very well over here, as you can see. And you?"

Fortunately we soon agreed to leave the café. Everything there was so narrow, stiff, and heavy, it just would not do. Outside it had begun to snow. Friedrichstrasse stretched white and empty before us. A few old-fashioned cars buzzed toward Unter den Linden. In front of a low house hung a sign inviting us to an exhibition of art from Inner Mongolia—a distant, alien, cold world. A sharp wind blew across the river.

"When we used to walk here, Vanya, do you remember?" I asked. "My God, what a crazy place this was, Friedrichstrasse near the railroad station. Nothing but little racketeers and pimps, nothing but streetwalkers—girls and guys—and a store every square yard: ties, ladies' lingerie, diamonds, betting shops, and sausage stands. This was a hot corner here, do you remember?"

Vanya barely seemed to be listening. He merely shrugged his shoulders, pushed a little snow aside with his shoes, and remained silent. We walked through Dorotheenstrasse up to the university, past the national library. It was an awkward and aimless walk—where to? We looked for a way back.

"But tell me," I said.

"What?" he asked. "What do you want me to tell you?"

"What happened to you that time?"

"Which time?"

"You know, that time at the People's Tribunal. They wouldn't let me attend the sentencing session."

Vanya made a dismissive gesture and once more shrugged his shoulders. Then he said, "Five years."

"Hmmm," I said, "pretty good. Five years of what?"

"Pen," he said, just "pen," and I remembered that in the language of prisoners that meant the penitentiary.

So he had been in the penitentiary, and now he began to remember, gradually began to tell his story. It was pretty terrible—the story of our times. He had been given five years for high treason, and Anni Korn had been given fifteen. No, it really had not been so bad. In those days they had actually longed to be sent to the penitentiary, for as long as you were in the hands of the judiciary, you were safe from the concentration camp. Their sentences had saved their lives. In 1945 they had both been liberated by the Red Army and had immediately begun participating in the reconstruction. Then they had studied sociology in Leipzig, married, and later joined the editorial staff of *Neues Deutschland*. And for the last two years he had had the honor of representing his newspaper in Cairo. He really said, "the honor."

So Vanya had become a Communist. I say this without any hint of accusation or of disgust, and without imbuing the word with the arrogant deviltry we tend to associate with the idea nowadays. I am simply stating the facts. He had fallen out of Hitler's Reich into the realm of the Soviets. For him the Red Army had been the liberator, and the Party was the great, delayed educator. His life must have been something like an education through German history: first the house behind Halensee Station, then Hitler, then the penitentiary, and then the new beginning granted by the

Russians—the Red Army as father and the Party as mother. After all, he had never had a real family. Now he put his faith in those who had showed concern for him: Vanya became the son of the Soviets. He embraced Communism with the fervor of a late convert. In 1947 he had joined the official party of East Germany, and now he was in possession of a truth he defended with grim zeal. He was a devout Marxist. The burden of his youth could not be relieved any other way. Wanting to survive, he had chosen the simple and evident way. The new state was his family; he was pledged to it. Now he was the one who was enslaved, and I could no longer follow him.

During this Christmas week we met twice more in East Berlin. Both attempts were fruitless; things between us became increasingly awkward. At bottom we had nothing left to say to each other. It was not his new faith—you can have great arguments with real Marxists—it was the banal and servile quality of that faith; everything was so pat. He espoused a limited and small-minded socialism that seemed crude and not thought through, as if read from scrolls. It was a superimposed, cramped Communism that exactly suited this cramped new Germany. Vanya was simply a mouthpiece of agitation and propaganda, supplanting reason with loyalty and arguments with enthusiasm.

He said, "The Red flag is flying on the moon."

116

I replied, "That's good, Vanya, but there are a couple of things that need to be done right here in East Berlin. The houses are pretty run-down—after twenty years."

He paid no attention. "Do you realize what that means? The moon has become a Soviet satellite. The stars course around Communism."

Later he spoke of imperialism and revanchism, of the headhunters and the morass of agents, and why would I not join him and his comrades? They stood for the Germany of the future. Everything he was saying was pretty awful, as cut-and-dried as a lecture over the radio. So I remained silent and grew increasingly disgusted.

At the end, when we were standing on the lower level of the Friedrichstrasse interurban stop and I was filled with sorrow, he said, "Trust me—socialism will win out."

Then I said, with some irony, fully aware of what I was saying, "All right, Vanya, you just go ahead and win out." And I never saw him again.

Time, time—how it colors everything, turns it yellow, dark, and slowly engulfs it: Herr Focken and Walter Flex, the perfect German boy; Vanya's balalaika and all those letters. All are almost forgotten. Time, they say, heals all wounds. But is that really true? Isn't it rather that time inflicts new wounds, wounds that never heal? Time covers everything like a mother with her apron, and one day we are grown up. Mother is gone, the apron has been withdrawn, and everything is still there: huge. My God, I'm no longer a child looking for miracles. My God, I'm no longer a young man in love with madness. There's an end to Hölderlin and Nietzsche in Eichkamp. Now I am a man with his memories, his peculiarities, his arrogance, his whiskey flask, and his advanced neuroses, and I cannot understand that this is what had to happen to us.

Vanya, it's over between us—of course. It's over for good. I ask you: What has made us such strangers? What can it have been? Once, in Berlin, we shared a desk in school where we learned the same grammar. I believe it is only time, Vanya, this mad, megalomaniac time, that swallowed us and vomited us up and spewed us out on alien shores. Now we both carry the stench of time: you smell of the East, and I smell of the West. That's how time spewed us out, that's all. We were engendered by vanquished and perplexed fathers, and our mothers were uneasy and without love. That sort of thing sticks, gets absorbed, itself becomes fate. Perplexity, emptiness, confusion were my youth, and yours was a mad, short dream. They simply did not give us anything that would stand up against time. Everything was only illusions and dreams; time had an easy game of it.

Vanya, we are a spoiled generation. We had no real family or home. So you chose the Party for your mother and the Red Army for your father, and I have nothing at all save my memories, my irony, and my advanced neuroses. I sit here in Frankfurt and write for the West—of course. And you sit in Cairo and write for the East—of course. Is it really a matter of course? It's a disgusting story, really, the very model of a cheap romance of German partition—out-and-out German junk. No one is interested in it any longer.

Why does life write such rotten stories? Two schoolboys from Berlin once joined together against Herr Focken and against Hitler and then were crushed and torn asunder during the Germans' great war—as was Germany herself—and they could not get back together.

In Custody

There's nothing I'm crazier about than mashed peas. Mashed peas is my favorite dish. You can serve it with bacon, with dried beef, with pigs' knuckles, or simply with bockwurst—it is always equally reliable. An honest German dish that palpably lets your stomach know it has received something of substance. Your whole body grows warm and firm. If you cook it with more liquid, it is called pea soup, and it is still worth a trip to Aschinger. Even in those days it was one of Berlin's highlights: pea soup with bacon and a lot of little rolls on the side. It cost forty-five pfennigs, and it was considered an honest German dish even without anything on the side. Mashed peas, more solid, was served with onions and sauerkraut and was eminently suited to cold winter days.

It was not a particularly cold winter day in December, and I was eating mashed peas. My body grew warm and firm from this venerable dish. I sat in our dining room at the heavy square table, which had been reduced to more modest proportions again after Ursula's death. It was a day like any other, Friday evening, just before eight o'clock. That afternoon I'd had a seminar on Plato at the university. The relationship of the True and the Beautiful had been Socratically examined. For two semesters now I had been studying philosophy. Recently I had been hearing a great deal about antinomies and aporias, and not just in Plato. My parents would not have understood; but they had kept my supper warm in the oven.

It had been cold on Friedrichstrasse station; I was frozen. In those days Berlin was very dark and drafty. The lights of the big city had been put out three months before; we were at war. At home, however, we were not particularly aware of it. I was eating mashed peas and bacon warmed up in the oven. Thick and hot, the food steamed in front of me; it was a grayish yellow and tasted a little of the oven. Our black grandfather clock struck eight. My mother and father were in the den discussing Christmas plans. It was to be our first wartime Christmas—Merry Christmas in the German campaign of self-defense. There was a lot to be discussed.

Suddenly the doorbell rang. It was astonishing to hear our bell at this hour. Eight o'clock was considered very late at our house, not far removed from bedtime. "I'm going," my father said crisply from the next room, indicating that he was determined to handle the unusual situation firmly. I heard him cross the hall, fumble with the key ring, open our safety lock, and speak with someone outside.

My head was filled with Plato, my mouth with mashed peas. I heard my father give a sharp, stifled cry. He came down the hall and threw open the dining-room door, displaying the large, intimidated face, the bewildered child eyes, of all civil servants. He stood trembling and questioning before me but said nothing. He spoke only with his eyes, which said, A person in need.

And like a workman in the factory canteen, I laid my spoon on the table, rose slowly—I was gangly and had grown much too tall for the house—and I thought, What can be so terrible at eight o'clock just before Christmas, while you're having your supper? I crossed the hall, and suddenly I saw Franz Bradtke standing in our doorway. White, snowy air billowed in from the darkness and framed Herr Bradtke, brisk and stiff as a green tin soldier.

I'd known him all my life. He was a calm, clumsy man with a brown walrus moustache, the very model of a village constable, and as children we looked up to him as we did to God the Father. But now Herr Bradtke was very officially wearing the tall, shiny helmet of all Berlin police officers, the strap pulled over his chin. Importance radiated from him; he was clearly on duty. Beside him, on a thick leather leash, a light-brown German shepherd was breathing heavily. Both filled the doorway, looming larger than life, glittering with snow like fearful fairy-tale figures, almost threatening to overturn our little house. Then I heard Herr Bradtke, who was still addressing me familiarly only a couple of years ago, calling me a lout and such, suddenly twang in a strange, disguised voice, "Come along, sir." After a while, when I merely stared at him, he repeated with great formality, "Let's go. Come along with me, young man." He said nothing more.

Thus began the end of our Eichkamp family, the family that collapsed so rapidly, the indestructible foundation of our moral world order. This Friday evening in the year 1939 marked the nullification of a German family that had, since August 1, 1914, sturdily and grimly fought against everything that was destructive and disintegrative in our country. Now they were taking away the last child. The house would be empty. And when I looked at Herr Bradtke with astonishment and perplexity and heard my mother calling from the den, "What is it? I am not at home," I knew at once: I must go with him now.

I went back into the hall, reached for my coat, looked for my gloves and a handkerchief because my mouth was still filled with mashed peas, and I thought: My dear parents. So the hour has arrived. They had come for me. The time of the beautiful lies is over, and your son is leaving you now. I know you have deserved better. I would like to have become what you hoped for—a civil servant perhaps, a good German citizen, a man with children and a beautiful wife and a real office in the city—something to be proud of. This much would have been your due. But things did not turn out that way. I am different. That's life. So a family dies, so it must fall apart. I go along.

Before my father had quite grasped the situation, I was closing the door behind me. Was I impelled outside? Snow whirled in the street, and many confused thoughts whirled through my head. Fear filled me, but something else as well— an absurd and bizarre sense of relief. So that's the way one leaves. That's how it is when the young leave their parents.

It was very pleasant to walk in the snow in Eichkamp. There were hardly any cars, and looking toward Grunewald we could see the fir trees, tall and dark, reach into the sky: winter peace in Prussia. We walked softly and noiselessly as across white carpets, and even the sound of policemen's boots was different here. It was already the third week of Advent, and much Christmas serenity lay over the houses. We met no one—except once, when a woman came along the road carrying a small Christmas tree under her arm. Herr Bradtke's boots crunched in the snow, giving our walk an official format. His footsteps echoed with his mission. He was silent, and even his dog breathed quietly on the way to the station house.

In Germany all police stations smell of cold smoke and leather, of the perspiration of small men, mixed with a little turpentine. They are painted gray; they are cold; they are furnished with wooden railings, wooden benches, and yellow wooden desk chairs; and there is always a portrait of the current ruler hanging on the wall. In those days, of course, it was a picture of our Führer. And behind the railings there are always records and forms that have to be filled out.

Herr Bradtke was working on a form. Sometimes, whenever a car was heard on the highway, he looked up expectantly. Then he calmed the dog, who had pricked up his ears, and went on writing. Once he shook his head. He had put his helmet aside, next to the inkwell. Now he was an official making a report; he was making a report to his superiors, and surely he used his best penmanship, rounding the upper loops and forcing the downstrokes. After every line he dipped his penpoint in the black ink. You could practically feel the effort exuding from such reports to superiors.

It seems that everything in a police station creaks: the policeman's boots creak, his joints, the floor of fibrous wood, and surely something creaks in his brain as the pen scrapes across the paper as slowly as a dull knife. Herr Bradtke did not say a word, but his breathing was audible. It was a heavy and rattling breath, a genuine police breath that age and tobacco and officialdom had made very pronounced. One can hear what takes place in a man's chest; nothing is hidden. Surely it's meant to be that way.

It was almost eleven before the others arrived. Doors slammed, and I heard male voices. Two police officers entered, saluted, laughed, and said, "Heil Hitler," bringing a lot of snow in with them. Then I was put in a vehicle called a Black Maria—a "Green Minna" in Berlin, for its outside really is green. It is a closed and windowless van, but on the inside there is a window between the driver's seat and the back section; iron benches run around the iron walls, and they let you sit on those. I was entirely alone and felt nothing but iron.

Finally the van started. It must have begun its rounds in Eichkamp, for then it crisscrossed Berlin, stopping at every precinct house and everywhere picking up whatever had been collected that night. A patchwork quilt of people accumulated. In Charlottenburg—I heard them call out the name—two fellows were loaded on who looked dangerous and had awesome bandages around their heads.

They grinned through slitted eyes and searched in their coat pockets for tobacco remnants. At the zoo station three girls were brought on board. They wore fur coats and lambskin boots and appeared very elegant. They were heavily rouged and also wished to smoke. They cursed vociferously, giggled, said to me, "Hey, Stretch, got a cigarette?" and laughed out loud some more. Then came three old men who said nothing at all, then a young man in an outlandish jacket, and then an old woman with tousled hair who muttered to herself and whispered, "I'm gonna let them have it, I will!" At Friedrichstrasse a handsome young man was pushed inside; the girls immediately addressed him as Fanny and seemed to know him well. Two Hitler Youths also stumbled in at a later stop, chained together at the wrists. They maintained a sulky silence.

By midnight the van was full. There was a smell of beer and rouge, of tobacco and perspiration. We were a wild heap, and we sometimes shriekingly tumbled across each other when the car braked suddenly. The van was a collection point for the dregs of a metropolis, a carful of riffraff such as can be found any night in any big city. I sat among them and thought, So here they drive the dregs around, nothing but the refuse of Berlin.

When, after many rattling curves, we finally

lurched to a halt, one of the girls called out snippily: "Moabit Prison, last stop." Everyone laughed, the doors were unbolted, and the crowd merrily hopped out—they almost seemed at home here. The old woman was cursing the guys with the bandages and pushing the handsome youth, who had a very la-di-da air and acted as if the whole vanload had nothing to do with him. The girls from the zoo district tripped carefully along and, once outside, spoke familiarly to the men in green.

Here in the courtyard it was dark and wet. Everyone was assigned a place, and when one of the policemen was about to send me along with the others, I suddenly heard an official grumble good-naturedly as he perused a list, "Nah, not that one, Charlie. He's a political. He goes to the Stapo."

Section 5, Cell 103. There was much to be learned. At five-thirty a piercing noise resounded through the corridors and staircases. Seven guards stood on seven floors, and an earsplitting concert of whistles ascended through an iron shaft. They blew the same kind of shrill whistles that had awakened numberless generations of Germans into heroic death, into battle, into trials; it was called the Great Awakening. This was followed by low-register shouting: bearded men's voices, emitting dark, hoarse sounds with all their might. High boots rang on cement floors, keys clattered, iron doors were pulled open and slammed shut again. Iron pounded on iron, and someone in the next cell shouted, "You pig!" They must have discovered him still on his cot. And once again keys clattered through the building.

This alarum lasted only a few minutes, and then the halls grew quieter. We awakened from dreams, from dark memories, from other times. Only a moment ago I was in the mountains in a blue meadow reading *Hyperion*. When I was still in school, I knew the poem by heart: "Now each morning I am on the heights of the Corinthian isthmus, and like the bee among flowers, my soul often flies back and forth between the seas which to the right and the left cool the feet of the gleaming mountains." And I went on speaking in the mountains, I went on speaking in Moabit Prison: "But what shall it serve me? The cry of the jackal who sings his savage dirge under the rock piles of antiquity startles me from my dreams. Happy the man whose heart is gladdened and strengthened by a flourishing fatherland."

The day was advancing, all Moabit was washing. The small gray enamel bowl into which we could pour water from a tall iron pitcher had already received the dirt of many prisoners—it would cleanse me this day as well. It did not take long. Tubs and heavy iron pots could be heard clattering through the halls. The invisible, lowly power of the trustees was approaching. They were like insects who have settled and made themselves at home in the building; they had power. The invisible, lowly army of insects came ever nearer with its heavy iron buckets; you could hear it moving and ringing and clanging. Soon the brown cell door would be harshly flung open, and outside two or three guys would be standing next to the guard. They looked smooth and pale and thin as young fishes, and they wore the blue-striped tunics of butchers' apprentices. You held out a brown enamel bowl, and with a small, long-handled ladle they slapped some black stuff into it; you could have dry bread as well.

The interrogations began at eight o'clock. You didn't notice anything, you just knew after a while. You could only listen while invisible men began to unlock cell doors with noisy zeal. Steps, calls, the slam of doors, a word of command, a whistle, then footsteps again, receding, then quiet. Oddly, every newcomer hoped for an interrogation. Everyone hoped that the steps were directed toward him, would come nearer, would stop at his door, that an eye would appear in the spyhole, that someone would turn the key in the lock and pull him out. It was a foolish and absurd hope. It fed on every sound.

At nine o'clock the sun slowly began to rise to our level. Today was a bright, clear winter's day, but the barred hatch overhead showed only a narrow blue stripe. From time to time they turned on heat that crackled and ticked in the realm of the floor-level pipes as warmth streamed upward; Prussia was good at heating. Now walking time began. Now Moabit Prison had its constitutional. Thousands of separate pedestrians paced back and forth along the five-step length of each prison cell.

It was the time of morning fantasies, of crazy hopes and dreams, rope ladders of great schemes and designs; they came and went like the steps outside. You had made up your mind, you had a plan, but you could not stick to it for long; you slid away from it like a glass on a tilted tray. Underneath perplexity lurked; fear rose from the heart and tugged at the left arm and on to the head. Then, outside, you suddenly heard the rattle of keys very close by, giving rise to hope—which was soon blasted. What next? Cell walkers are like lost mountain climbers: the path keeps on, upward and downward, with heights and ravines. In the end, they were back where they started.

By ten the sun had moved so far into the room that the walls began to speak. Prison walls all over the world tell unutterable stories; they are the slates of those who have been struck dumb. With the handles of spoons they have etched their hopes and fears into obdurate surfaces. As in public lavatories, the nightmares of the lower depth are vis-

131

ible there, and these were obscene. "Drop dead, Hitler," someone had written way down by the floor, next to a sketch of a naked woman. "Hail Moscow," it said three times over in a circular ribbon around a hammer and sickle directly under the woman. Someone had tried to scratch it out and had carved a cross on top of it, with the words *Ora pro nobis*. And of course, all prisoners keep a calendar. There are always six little downstrokes standing close together like hatch marks; then comes a longer stroke—Sunday—and when the week is over, a line is drawn through the whole thing and a new series of little strokes is started. You could clearly read how much time each one spent here, for suddenly one of those strokes broke off, leaving the week unfinished.

Invariably at one o'clock they brought dinner. Why does food in prison always taste so much of prison? How do they do it? "There's saltpeter in it. It cools down your sex drive," they said, laughing. But there was surely also sweat and fear and poverty in it—you could taste Prussian administration. They served mostly peas—an honest German dish—but they spoiled it in a disgusting way: peas in water used to boil potatoes, peas in sauerkraut water, or just plain peas. On Sundays they added a piece of meat, which the butcher's apprentices slapped on your plate with their masturbators' fists, quick as a flash. This too tasted not of meat

132

but of prison meat—that is, guilty meat. "They spoil everything here with their saltpeter," they said, laughing. "You'll have to get used to it." All flesh was guilty here.

In the afternoon, around three o'clock, renewed activity descended upon the building. The business with the keys started all over again. Names were called out once more, people were led past, work units were assembled, keys clattered through the corridors. The man next door to you was chosen—a lucky case, they've just come for him—and when the three of them walked past you, the smell of wonderful freedom walked with them. Why him? Why not me? There were so many puzzles in prison, and there was no solution for any of them.

Five o'clock in the afternoon. Moabit was a beehive of activity. Now enemies of the state were interrogated, questioned, examined, and confronted with other enemies of the state. Tell us one more time, confess, we know all about it. Records were drafted and documents were dictated. As early as 1929 I was a member of the Pacifist League, yes; in those days I was an instigator, a member of the Communist party; I hired Jews in my business, I always voted for Ebert, but I am loyal to the new state. My son is in the Hitler Youth, I did not want it to happen. I know nothing, nothing at all. These statements wafted through the whole building, known and ignored, noticed and laughed away: Man, you expect us to believe that? No one is a hero until afterward. Everyone wants to live. Man is a bundle of hope and fear. He lies, of course he lies.

Evening came quickly and turned rapidly into night. Why did one always sleep so well in prison? Night was dense and black—it could not be taken into custody by policemen. Soundlessly it seeped through the walls from outside. Like a mother, like a woman, night came and spread over all the world, a little obscene and opening out on nothingness. This attracted us, sucked us in; we came, we fell, we drowned. Night was the great forgetting. You could still hear keys, heavy iron footsteps, an occasional cry in the next cellblock, but these sounds grew less frequent, receded, softened, ebbed, became submerged, themselves became dreamlike and unreal. By nine o'clock, no later, Moabit Prison had become a nightmare I left behind. I was free again, I was on the outside, I was dreaming. You could not put night in chains.

Sleep was the freedom of all prisoners. They allowed it. It was what they still let us have. We could forget. I would dream of wonderful worlds, of a blue meadow in the mountains, where I would be reading *Hyperion* again: "Like the laborer into refreshing sleep, so sinks my troubled self often into the arms of the innocent past. The rest of childhood! Heavenly rest! How often I stand quietly before you in loving contemplation and wish to summon you."

Thus I abruptly found myself between the millstones of history and barely knew how it had happened. Overnight I had become an enemy of the state, though I had so little talent for the part. All I had done was to spend my evenings with Vanya and deliver those letters, and now I was enmeshed in the most terrible predicament of my whole life.

I will never forget it. I learned the story only gradually. The predicament was called high treason, and it seemed to have spread itself like an underground plague through the whole country. My case was called "Preliminaries Concerning an Action for High Treason Against the Writer Broghammer and Others," and these others were a hundred and one people, all of whom were arrested on the same night. I did not know them. I knew only Vanya, who was an insignificant appendage to Anni Korn, who in her turn was an insignificant appendage to someone else, and that someone had dangled from another, and that other from still another, according to the classical rules of conspiracy. That is how one had to work in the underground. Now all of them were stuck here and were being interrogated, one by one.

135

They interrogated me at length as well, at least in the beginning. They did not beat me and dunk me in cold water, as they did others. They did not put me in solitary or dislocate my arm, as they did others. When they questioned me, they sat across the table very properly and attentively. They had good German names like Müller and Dr. Stein and Krause II, they smoked cigarettes, they said please and thank you and addressed me as Mister, and surely they realized quite soon that they had not caught anything substantial when they caught me—nothing on which to build a solid political case.

A safe held a thick file about me which both astonished and relieved me in an unexpected way. They had kept tabs on my mail for almost a year, intercepting all the letters I got, opening them, photographing them, and then sealing them up again and sending them on to me. I had never noticed a thing. These letters, now existing in photocopies on the left-hand side of the ledger and in a typewritten version on the right, became my salvation.

What kind of letters are written by a boy from Eichkamp at the age of nineteen, the son of unpolitical parents, a middle-class boy, a philosophy student with a penchant for Hölderlin and Nietzsche, and what kind of letters will he get? The letters were pretty eccentric and crazy—outpourings of friendship, epistles of sorrow, hymns of rapture and excitement, messages of loneliness, and celebrations of the soul—O Hyperion—cast off stutteringly and carelessly. It was the typical adolescent drivel of nice young men of nineteen in the Germany of those days. This sentimental hodgepodge eschewed the ground floor of world history and soared to the top, hung like tinsel of the soul in the fly loft of German rapture. It was derived from a superficial knowledge of Schiller and Fichte, uplifted by Novalis and Wackenroder, transported by Rilke and Hesse. All of it was fairly embarrassing and adolescent. There was just one thing it wasn't, and that was political.

Yes, it was all very German and spiritual, and it conferred on me the image of the seeker and idealist who had taken one false step. In those days I must have been a terribly muddled fellow, a typical German youth whose head was filled with beauty, with death and madness, and somewhere they had a remnant of respect for that sort of thing. It was not really strange to them, only too elevated. Soon enough they entered me in the ranks of the victims, of the dreamers and visionaries. I was a victim of the counterrevolution, a victim of Vanya and his friend Anni. So said Herr Krause II one night after a long interrogation, patting my shoulder. I did not contradict him, not ever. I thought, That may be my way out of here.

And I thought, Actually, it's the truth. We've always been unpolitical at our house.

After three months they moved me to another cellblock, and I became part of the permanent population; probably they thought they'd made my life easier. The configuration was entirely new; I had drifted from Eichkamp into a solid block of politicals. Citizens of Eichkamp did not do time in Moabit. These men were all Communists, trade unionists and other Reds, who had engaged in protest. There were Poles and other enemies of the Reich, Czechs and other enemies of the Protectorate; there were Jews, people closely related to Jews, lackeys of Jews and other enemies of the state. There were radio criminals, who had secretly listened to broadcasts from Strasbourg or Basel and talked about them; currency criminals, who had taken Reichmarks abroad; economic criminals, who had bought a quarter of a pound of liverwurst "without," thus undermining Germany's war economy. Then there were boycott instigators, fault-finders, and intellectuals, who had sinned through derogatory remarks against the treason law; wicked tellers of jokes, who also undermined; and still others who were enemies of the Reich on general principle. In those days the whole world was full of enemies, full of inferior people, ferrets and bloodsuckers who were determined to sabotage our poor, proud country. Here in Moabit I came to know them.

And I came to know prison, the world of prisoners, the language of imprisonment, the rites of resignation and hope, prisoners' rituals: kneading chessmen from bread, smoking without letting the smell escape, the rapping alphabet, passing notes, making playing cards from old paper bags, exhausting the pleasures of hall duty, getting information while shaving, talking without moving your lips during walks in the courtyard.

Prison communication is a miserable and sophisticated art nourished by signs on doors and walls, by the most delicate sounds. It scrabbles together tobacco scraps and straw, listens long at cell doors, learns to distinguish the most indistinguishable sounds, and for a while makes you throw yourself at every newcomer, crushing him as if he carried the secrets of the whole world under his jacket—Tell me, what's new? Go on, speak up, how are things on the outside? Every new man is a hope that flickers, shines briefly, and then dies down before slowly turning into dull brooding. The new one is from another cellblock, has been here almost a year and displays the crafty features of a smalltime sharpie. He demands butts and trades them for farfetched rumors: We're going to be transferred, you'll see; a commission is arriving tomorrow; starting in April there's going to be tobacco; C Wing had health inspection yesterday; next week the old ones will be transferred to Tegel; the politicals are going to be put in Prinz Albrecht Strasse, the others can get work at Siemens; and so on. These stories seep through cracks and keyholes, spread like wildfire through the corridors, move into other cells, cling to the walls for a time, then flake off and quickly disintegrate. Rumor is the daily newspaper of prisoners.

Every Friday the shifts changed in Moabit. That was when the hard cases were mustered out and taken away to be softened up. Roll call was as early as two o'clock. Everybody out, line up, stop, stand at attention. The squad leader reported to the guard, the guard to the doorkeeper, the doorkeeper to the watch captain, and he in turn to the warden. After a time some gentlemen arrived, high officials, it seemed, in splendid business suits—the commissars of the secret police. They ordered lists to be read out. They did not do it themselves; they only stood by silently, and sometimes they grinned when they heard a name that meant something to them. Bethke, Karl—step forward. You see, Bethke, you could have spared yourself all this, isn't that right? Did Bethke agree? They had so many methods here; they did not dirty their hands. Men who did not offer up anything substantial although they had it to give—

like Bethke, for example—were taken to Oranienburg for six weeks, for special treatment by the SS. They would be kneaded into softness. Then we'd see.

At six o'clock in the evening the cars returned, bringing those they had taken away six weeks before: Bense, Hermann; Meister, Kurt; Schuhmacher, Horst. And Levi, Siegfried, who had been just as taciturn as the others and so had also merited six week's kneading to make him nicely pliant and sociable. Berlin's Moabit Prison was almost a rest cure; everyone wanted to be here. Now he would talk—tell everything.

It was gloomy in the cell. It was a dreary March day, and by six o'clock it was almost dark. Snow was dripping outside as Levi, Siegfried, was delivered. A thin, brownish light burned above the cell door. I watched the short man stumble over the threshold, stand fearful and perplexed near the wooden cots, and ask politely, "Where may I sit down, gentlemen?" Silence, laughter, snorting in the room—had there ever been anything like it? *Gentlemen?* At night he lay by my side and kept on asking, "Do they beat you here too—with those horsewhips?" And after a pause I told him no, I knew nothing about that, and I pushed some bread his way, an old, dried-up crust I still had under my pillow. "Eat something," I said softly. "You must be half starved, man."

At that, Levi, Siegfried, began to whimper, breathed deeply, suddenly started panting convulsively; the panting soon turned into sobbing, and then there was an outburst. The short, bald man who used to own a jeweler's shop under the Bülow Arch and who always remained a gentleman, even in Oranienburg, broke into loud, childish weeping. He wailed and moaned to himself, "Now they'll come and beat me again. You're not allowed to eat out of turn—don't you know that, sir?" It was enough to make you laugh; it was very funny, this episode with the strange Herr Levi. He gave us many more occasions for laughter.

One day my parents came to visit. In Moabit such a message is terrible and wonderful. It made me downright sick. They took me from my cell, they led me along iron corridors down three circular staircases, then along still more corridors of iron. Then there was a big fence, actually a cage, through which they shoved me. Papers were signed, and a civilian took charge of me and guided me through many more halls, this time with wooden doors and floors of linoleum. There was a smell of turpentine. I walked stiffly and rigidly, pulling my shoulders up like a wooden marionette, keeping my hands clutched behind my back, acting as if none of it had anything to do with me, and thinking, Your parents are here—didn't you hear? What brings them to your prison? How did they get in?

The civilian did not take me to a visitor's cell but to his office cubicle. My parents were of a slightly higher class, after all, and so that's where they were put. I was startled. They had come a long way. They were sitting in high-backed chairs, fearful, touching, and somehow hysterical with love. They seemed so elegant. My mother wore a shiny fur coat, a silky dress, and pearls around her throat. This was her standard operagoing outfit. She opened a cardboard suitcase on the floor, and as always, amazingly, she had thought of everything—socks and underpants and a white nightshirt. Now she stumbled over them as she hugged me, exclaiming, "My son, my poor son." And then she began to cry properly, as she did at the opera. They had brought my suitcase from Eichkamp, all those little artifacts of the past: a shaving kit and handkerchiefs, a towel, some writing material, many heavy socks—even *Hyperion*. Here I recognized them as mine.

And I wanted to write a letter. "It was really nice of you to come and see me. I thank you for all the good things. I'm sure they won't let me keep them—but all the same. And best regards to you, from your son." It would have read something like that. But it did not work out like that. They were here, they were really in the room, and I had to say something. Not all of it, just something. How did you do that? My father looked very thin and old; he gazed at me with those big, disturbed child's eyes, the eyes of all civil servants, and he kept whispering, "The minister, the minister, I spoke to the minister about your affairs. You'll soon be free." And then he gulped to make me look away. It was a correct family scene, like in the Bible: the prodigal son—or rather, the prodigal parents. This sort of story can be worked out. It has a happy ending most of the time; it isn't always necessary to slaughter the fatted calf. Love is everlasting—you can read it on many a gravestone. Return, my son, all is forgiven.

"Commissar, sir," I heard my mother say after a time. She had turned beseechingly to the Gestapo official with a compelling theatrical gesture. She was still an unusual and impressive woman who fairly glittered; at one time she wanted to be an opera singer, and some of that stuck. "Commissioner, sir, our son is innocent!" she said authoritatively. "Believe us, we know him well. We have always been unpolitical, believe me." And my father too had risen to his feet. "Never," he said, "has there been anything of that sort in our family—high treason. Impossible, in our family."

My God, it was all so touching and kindhearted. Now they stood before the official like two broken angels and pleaded for their son. My God, they were still dreaming the same old family dream, still clinging to the fairy tale that began in 1914 on August 1, the day war broke out, the day they were married. They wanted to cover the rupture with love. They wanted to stuff the crack in the world with family: our family, our son, our house. My dear ones, isn't all of that broken and scattered?

It was horrible. At such elevated moments my feelings always congealed; I grew cold, motionless, and unable to speak. Only when I was alone did life return to me. I thought, They will go home, sad yet comforted; they will take their seats in the interurban train, perplexed and silent. They no longer understand their son, who is now doing time among nothing but politicals—after all, we were always entirely unpolitical. As they walk through the empty house, the boards will creak. Everything will be still and hard, but they will go on hoping for the happy ending. They are so good. They are like agitated children lying in wait behind the windowpane of an evening, expecting a miracle. Everyone always expects a miracle. It will not happen. The play is over, the script has run its course, the stage is empty—and you still wander about, my dear ones. Now you sit in Eichkamp and I in Moabit Prison, you in your cottage and I in my cell. And that is the end, the last of a good German family.

The night of decision had arrived. The preliminary examination by the secret police had been completed. Everyone knew that when the proceedings reached this point, they were passed on to the examining magistrate. He was the one who had to decide, to call in each separate prisoner and determine whether the records that had been accumulated warranted transmittal to the state attorney's office with a request to bring charges. It could also happen that they let you go. They liked sticking to this judicial procedure. It lent an appearance of legality to the whole business. Justice is something you can juggle most wonderfully.

It was the beginning of April, and I was already fast asleep. Shortly after midnight they came to get me. They rousted me out of bed and shouted, "Go on, hurry. Hurry up, you. Are you asleep, or what?" Locks were snapped and keys jangled with great haste and officiousness. Then another walk through iron corridors, through cellar passages, through heavy armored doors that were cumbersomely opened and barred again. The high boots of the men in green rang loudly on the stone floor, echoing importance. I was no longer stiff; the rigidity had left me. I thought, Everything in Moabit is asleep, but something has awakened in your affair. Now something is going to happen, something is going to change.

They led me through a Stygian labyrinth, a veritable subterranean realm, a murky city within a city. It went on interminably, then wound around still another corner, and suddenly I stood in a dark hallway and was prevented from going further. Two men in green held me tight, planting themselves sturdily on either side of me. We stood along a wall, and after a while I discerned other prisoners and other men in green who had also been standing there.

Gradually my eyes grew accustomed to the dim light. I saw a long, gloomy basement passageway with prisoners lined up along both sides. They stood as if they had been nailed there, and between every two prisoners stood a policeman, in an endless chain disappearing somewhere in the shadows. They had brought together all the accused in the criminal case against the writer Broghammer and others. I did not know them. This was the first time I had seen their faces, and in them I beheld the other, the secret Germany. It looked pale and confused and adventurous; it was a gathering of underground men.

Enemies of the state bore a surprising resemblance to each other. They looked wretched and fearsome, their suits were much too loose and ragged, their faces were emaciated and bearded; sometimes a last flicker of life twitched in their spent eyes. Darkness spread around them. It was hard to believe that these were the heroes of the resistance, who were always described to us as such brave and shining figures—they were not like that. Rather, they were like partisans in a war—ragged, starved, with an aura of crime and guilt clinging to them. They were very isolated and wore no uniform that might protect them. Now each wore his deed alone; each had become guilty for himself alone. Once they might have been journalists and writers—now they were only criminals. Once they might have been students and professors—now they were only leftovers, victims, broken vessels of power. There was no point in boasting of them.

The chain inched forward very slowly, from time to time moving by a couple of yards. At the very front was a door, and when it was opened a ray of light spilled out, quickly swallowing up one man. A bright globe of light encircled his form, shone on it sharply for a moment, pulled it inside. Then the door fell shut. Darkness enveloped the corridor once more. Then waiting, standing, silence, and another push forward. Slowly the wall I faced was illumined again, and a tall, stocky man with tousled hair and a beard materialized before me. He looked like a gypsy or a professor from Bohemia; his tongue slid over his lower lip, and then he bit it. Like an ancient tree he stood between the two policemen who, brisk and young, flanked him like green foresters. They had captured the game.

Suddenly an intense glare flooded over me. I

was in the room of the examining magistrate. I stumbled a little—everything here was as warm and bright as day. The room was bare and empty except for a stack of files piled high on a desk. The man behind the files looked old and wrinkled, tiny and mousy. He wore rimless golden pince-nez and kept looking in the file and then back at me, comparing this and checking that and sinking down over his desk, reading and mumbling to himself. I was standing very close to the desk, and right before me I could see two high piles of paper. They were forms I recognized—two stacks of preprinted blanks, one green, the other bright red. Turning my head a little to one side, I blinked, and on the red pile I could make out PROSECUTE! and on the green one DISMISS!—thick black letters followed by an exclamation point. Suddenly the blood began to pound in my throat—the word *dismiss* existed, had suddenly appeared. I never believed I would see it here, but there it was, squatting big and fat on the green paper, and it pulsed in my throat and danced through the room and whirled through my head. All you have to do now is keep quiet and wait, something in me said. He must reach for a piece of paper, he must decide between red and green. In the end, that's what he had to do.

Suddenly he started to question me. He wanted to know about my relationship with Vanya—why, and to what purpose, and how long. And I said, "Always, since we were in school. He was just my friend."

"Your evaluation isn't bad," he replied, pointing with his pencil at the files. "You come from a decent family. How could you seek out such friends?"

I shrugged my shoulders and said, "I don't know. It just happened that way."

He sank back in his chair, and after a while, without looking up, he said, "Do you know the opinion our colleagues formed about you?"

I remained silent, and he abruptly resumed. "I will read it to you: 'With proper treatment, may possibly still be salvaged for the people's state.'" After a pause during which he laid his pencil across his lips and looked at me critically, he continued. "Well, what do you have to say about that? Is it true, do you think?"

I merely nodded and stared at the two piles of paper, green and red, thinking, Which one will he reach for? Perhaps green—with proper treatment? Suddenly a paralyzing fear took hold of me, the fear that it would go on like this forever, always examinations and interrogations, always cells and locks—you won't get out, you're stuck—and I saw him reach for the red pile, and softly I said, "Let me out of here, sir—for the love of God."

Time passed. He looked at me searchingly and

meditatively, suddenly pushed the files away, rose, bent forward; only now was it evident that he was a very short man. With his right hand he reached for a pile, pulled out a green form, said nothing at all, and began to write.

I am free, I am free—I could barely believe it. What is it, freedom? A smell, a taste, a breath of the world, everything. I inhaled deeply; it was April, and there was a hint of spring in the air. I walked through the streets of the city, walked in a daze past stores, restaurants, vegetable carts with cabbages and oranges. I heard a woman shout, I watched a boy pulling a cart, I looked in shopwindows, I saw myself in a mirror—so that's who you are, you are free, here you go. I felt cement under my feet, gray and wet; a dog sniffed a lamppost, and cars came toward me along the road. I heard the interurban train slogging along high overhead; bright and quick, the yellow train strained past. People rushed by. I was so greedy for the world now that I could taste the world again—gray, dim, ugly Berlin, its walls and railroad arches, its bridges and bars. I read *Schultheiss-Patzenhofer*, I read *Singer*, I read *Brauhaus Tempelhof*. Everything had come back to me, like a gift. Freedom—that is a world in which we can lose and find ourselves.

Now you must absorb the old words and gestures all over again. You are free. You must learn again to reach into your pants pocket, to pull out your wallet, to open it, to look for coins. You had it all once, but you have to acquire it again. At the Friedrichstrasse railroad station you must step up to the ticket window and you must say out loud, "Eichkamp, one way, third class." You must say it very calmly. No one is to realize that it is new to you and that you are going at it for the first time. You used to do it in the old days. Everything will be as it once was.

As always, I went to Aschinger and stood at the counter, surrounded by people. I went to the end of the line. A fat woman was dishing out soup at the head of the line. I was hungry—hungry for the world and hungry for pea soup—and I heard myself say, "Pea soup with bacon." Then I went off with my bowl to stand at one of those tables, breathing heavily and thinking, There's nothing better than peas. Peas is my favorite dish.

I stood at the ticket counter in Friedrich-strasse station and heard myself saying clearly, "Eichkamp, one way, third class." It sounded foreign to me. A woman tossed a yellow ticket at me—women are working everywhere now—and coins rolled across the brass plate, turned over, pitched down, tumbled to the floor. I stooped and picked them up hurriedly, feeling my fingers tremble as I did; I grasped the piece of yellow cardboard and ran away, and then I was standing on the escalator, letting it carry me slowly upward. Up above, nothing had changed. The green shield was displayed: Spandau-West. My God, I'd been in Moabit Prison, but all the time trains left for every corner of Berlin. How could that be? Where was time? Where had it gone?

So I would go to Eichkamp. As always, I would sit in the train compartment while the houses and walls and streets of the city flew by the window—an ancient melody. Zoo, Savigniplatz, Charlottenburg, Westkreuz, Eichkamp. I would get off the train there, walk through the settlement, and come to a stop at our house—of course. I would ring the doorbell and wait, my heart beating, and I would say, "Here I am," feeling a little awkward. My mother would hug me with an elegant, somewhat theatrical gesture, and she would sob, "My child, my son, my dear child." And I would stand there stiff and rigid, thinking, I am here.

Was I here?

1945: Zero Hour

Final memory of his Reich: an act of protest. We had dug holes with shovels, with spades and hoes, and we cowered in them like sidewalk trees waiting to be planted the following day. We lay along the Dortmund-Ems Canal. We were charged with holding the Ruhr sector. We huddled in deep, damp, sticky holes as a light drizzle fell. We were called Combat Group Grasmehl, and we were what was left of a paratroop regiment, a hundred or so men from Brandenburg, hurriedly drummed up in the final days. Actually we were from a convalescent unit. We were nothing but the sick, the wounded, the disabled—invalids between two postings. We had hardly any weapons; instead we had bandages around our abdomens and our thighs, adhesive tape on our backs, printed diet lists in our pockets. Combat Group Grasmehl, enlisted in the battle against the USA.

In Brandenburg they told us, "You are being transferred, you'll be taken to a convalescent home." Many freight cars were lined up at the railroad platform, an endless train of brown, rusty cars. We were loaded on with baggage and marching rations, a few weapons thrown in, but then nothing happened. No locomotive. That puzzled me. All morning I squinted suspiciously along the platform and kept an eye out for a locomotive. I told myself, That's important now. It will decide your fate. The ring around his Reich has become pretty tight, Greater Germany is contained between the Oder and the Rhine, and if the engine is hooked up from the direction of Berlin, they are sending us against the Russians. You'll be toiling in Russia for a long, long time. But if it comes from the direction of Magdeburg, we're heading for the Americans. I had few ideas to go with that concept—almost none.

In the late afternoon—I was dozing in my corner—the train suddenly lurched. A hard thud, the hum of iron, squeaking, a rattle as of a rusty chain being pulled tight; we were underway. I leaped up and looked outside; we were moving west. Good. Westward, ho!

In Unna they took us off. As we marched through the town, we passed some barracks. This was where the SS was quartered, and when they heard our tired, dragging march, they came rushing, flying to the windows with scared, searching looks. SS men with large, frightened eyes, their coats unbuttoned, some in the midst of washing, had rushed to the windows in their undershirts; one was holding a razor as if to conjure with it, shaving foam around his lips. But no, not at all, we must have looked familiar; we were not the Americans—yet. There was still time. They could retreat to the rear. This was my first shock after so many years: the SS was afraid, the SS was in flight.

It was our task to provide cover for the retreat of the SS units at the Dortmund-Ems Canal. That was why we were sitting there in those clay holes, and that was why we were given great quantities of cookies and beer and cigarettes. New weapons was what we were not given. The others had them. On the opposite shore nothing could be seen but gray, rutted fields, March land. But somewhere in the back country they must have brought up enormous quantities of cannons and heavy weapons, and with these they bombarded and currycombed our positions yard by yard. Three or four times a day it broke over our heads: a hurricane of fire and steel, stones and spurting soil. Were we to throw beer bottles against all that? Sometimes a voice cried out, sometimes parts of bodies flew through the air. Then calm returned. Someone whimpered in the next foxhole, and a motorcycle came driving up; the wounded man was pulled out, and a new man was stuck in the hole. That's how it was done. That's how we passed four days and nights.

On the fifth day I was detached from the unit. A motorcycle messenger drove up and shouted something in my ear. As of that moment, I was assigned to food-supply liaison. Had I heard correctly? I allowed some time to pass, rose, feeling stiff as a board, and crawled back through wet grass past ruins and uprooted streets.

Behind the skeleton of a building I stood upright and regained my senses. It must have been a school at one time, for shiny desks were scattered across the field.

Schoolyard feelings. I sat down at one of the desks and breathed deeply, looking up at the sky that hung overhead gray and damp as a sheet. I thought: Easter. That's right, today is Easter Sunday. My God, there used to be such a thing, a real Easter. You got up early and put on your Sunday finery, went to church, looked for eggs in the garden—red ones, blue ones, green ones—then drank coffee in the dining room. On the radio they quoted Goethe's "Freed from the Ice," and afterward Elly Ney played something significant by Beethoven.

Now all of that was finished. No more Goethe and Beethoven, no resurrection. Now all the guns of the world were trained on Germany. The end had come, the real end of the world, as it was foretold in the Bible. The Reich was falling apart—his Reich, our Reich—the German Reich was falling apart. Now dying was all that was left to us. Thank God, the German Reich was finally falling apart.

At the provisioning center they acted as they did in all the provisioning centers on earth. They always survived the end of the world. A basement, corridors in semidarkness, cubicles, counters, warning signs, a regimental proclamation still fluttering on a blackboard. A stout private first class squatted lazily behind his cans like a grocer. He had a pencil stuck behind his ear like a store clerk, and after some chitchat he affected condescending indifference as he doled out bread and bologna and a huge clump of margarine. Cigarettes on top of that, jam in addition, bottles of beer. I pushed everything deep into my canvas satchel, tossed it across my back as if it were a sack, and trotted back.

Some fog and damp was already rising from the ground. Though it was barely five o'clock, it was nearly dusk again. Somewhere in the distance a machine gun burped. I sank into the slippery, clayey soil. Right next to the ruined schoolhouse was our bunker. Something resembling a company command post had been improvised here for Combat Group Grasmehl. In a shell of a building, its interior walls stretching naked to the sky, was a kind of orderly room. Two sergeants sat around churning nervously on a field telephone. "Hello, can you hear us? Combat Group Grasmehl calling. Hello, is this Division HQ?"

I delivered my provisions and tried something approximating a salute. I never could succeed in making it appear very soldierly, but the two at the telephone no longer cared very much. They said, "All right, get out of here," as if they were talking to a dog. They ignored my wretched civilian manners. That was a clear sign; when German sergeants become human, you can bet your life a world war has been lost.

Outside, behind the house, abruptly the deep shock. I have not forgotten it to this day, I shall never forget it. There stood Hermann Suhren against a wall, looking almost like Jesus. They had removed his belt buckle, torn off his private-first-class stripes, and tied a white cloth around his eyes. He looked like a wounded soldier whose head had just been bandaged—and indeed he had been wounded.

A year ago in Cassino, along with me, also at Eastertime—Easter of 1944—we had both been wounded in the first assault on Hill 503, just below the monastery. We had met again in the military hospital in Bozen, and later, in Germany, we had become friends. A week ago we had come here together from Brandenburg. Hermann was a watchmaker and had been born somewhere around here, on Westphalian soil. He was Catholic in that dull and loyal manner one often sees in young men from Westphalia, and he was thus immune to the grim fanaticism of those eager to fight to the bitter end. "Man," he said to me repeatedly, "when it starts going wrong—oh, my God."

Now they were about to shoot him. A paratroop lieutenant stood twenty yards away from me, two noncommissioned officers at his side. The lieutenant had strapped his submachine gun across his shoulder and hip. I did not know him, I'd never seen him before, but he looked slender and blond and wiry, like all the world's lieutenants. I was just about to rush between them—"Hermann, what is it, what are they doing to you? This can't happen, it must be a mistake"—when I heard the bright bark of the submachine gun, a stray report. Only five or six shots, very quick, very tight and precisely aimed, and I saw Hermann Suhren silently collapsing along the wall. Slowly he sagged like a flour sack; he doubled over, fell headfirst into the mud, made impact but made no sound. I knew, bullets were a painless way to die. All you feel is a dull thud, nothing more.

Later I learned a few details. Hermann had crawled away from his hole and had been missing from his post for half a day; he had disappeared behind this ruined house. To this day I have no idea whether he was simply looking for a safe

160

place—a sensible military precaution against the hurricane of falling iron—or was no longer prepared to continue fighting. His native village was not, after all, very far away. At the time everything was already close to the final stage; the war was approaching chaos, the confusion of nothing but rearguard positions, isolated people, stragglers, deserters. Some men went on grimly fighting, some still believed in the victory, and in between everyone tried to save his own skin.

But someone had caught Hermann. One of those blond, Nordic gods whom the war had begotten and exalted had caught him sleeping in the ruins of the building, about three hundred yards behind the front. He had turned it into a case of absence without leave from the unit, a case of cowardice in the face of the enemy, a case of desertion, and he had given the culprit short shrift. This was permitted. There were such orders in those days, crazy orders from the morose man in Berlin, designed to maintain the discipline and fighting morale of the troops. Yes, the action was all but legal; toward the end any officer could shoot down any soldier who was fleeing.

But for me this was the moment when I awoke, when I started up out of four years of soldier's sleep, when I said, It is finished, it is the end, you will not spend another day among this people. It was my moment of truth. Suddenly I was entirely filled with anger and hate and protest. Hermann, they have killed you, my friend from Cassino, my friend from Westphalia. They have shot millions of people, all of us have pulled the trigger, all our hands are covered with blood. Europe is a bloodbath, Fortress Europe is a slaughterhouse; little by little all of us are shooting down all of us. The war has become revolting, senseless carnage, as revolting as our German mythology: the bloody battlefield, King Atli's death and Kriemhild and Siegfried and grief over Valhalla.

Oh, this people, of whom I am one! What is it about them, these people who let themselves be butchered so bloodily, who at the last minute shoot and stab, murder and bludgeon their own? I hate this people of Nibelungen faith shot through with the trait of heroic grandeur, this band of killers with the brooding face of Richard Wagner, these comrades in slaughter who here, on the stage of history, disguised as generals and judge advocates, play out the ancient German epic, the Götterdämmerung.

I did not want to be a German anymore. I wanted to leave this people. I was about to change sides.

I know all that sounds a little vainglorious. It was five minutes to twelve, and the nation was collapsing like a house of cards, having endured a mere seventy years. They divided up the pieces at

Yalta. In Berlin the powerful men had for weeks been carrying around little ampules that they would bite through when they came to the end of their hellish ride through history. In four weeks they would bite. At this moment, when everywhere the nightmare was lifting, when even the blind could see again, you changed sides—you, a petty little private first class in the German army, twenty-five years old, one among twenty million in uniform. All alone you crossed your Rubicon and stepped up to the United States of America and said, "I don't want to go on, I can't go on. I come out of hatred for Hitler and out of rage and desperation about my people."

This damned German loyalty! I know that my attitude came a little late, almost smacked of pushiness. In fact it was no longer possible. I should have gone under with them. The Americans would only grin and say, "Look at them, those Germans—now they come crawling one by one and claim that they were always opposed. A disgusting people, all thoroughly servile. Now, when antifascism is being hawked in the world's marketplaces at bargain prices, now they betray their own cause. A base display of treachery."

All the same, in those days I changed sides. I was filled with hatred, I was startled out of the lethargy of my soldier's life. I was wide awake, and I was saying to myself, Now something has to

163

happen. Now you have to act. Now you can't go along anymore.

I crawled back into my hole. Night had already fallen over the Dortmund-Ems Canal. I slid right into the mud, let myself fall, reached for my carbine, got it cocked and ready, and was prepared to shoot. It was a senseless action, for we were sitting ducks and for the last two days had had no ammunition. Sometimes, when the enemy released flares, it was suddenly bright as day, and for a few seconds everything looked like a battlefield in a provincial production of *Macbeth*. Why did the end of the world have this veneer of provincial staging? Was it because world history is, at bottom, a Puccini opera?

Next to me in the hole cowered a new guy. A young kid, around twenty, intelligent peasant face, black mop of hair, which I saw when he took off his steel helmet right in the middle of the firing. Was he crazy? In the middle of the grenade explosions he set up a tiny pocket mirror, reached into his pocket for a comb, wet it with saliva, and started to fix his hair. He cared for nothing but the part in his hair, preened like a gigolo getting ready for a heavy date in front of his bathroom mirror. Narcissus in Germany's final battle.

My God, put your helmet back on, hurry up. Shrapnel was flying around like flies in summer. Leave your face alone—your looks won't last much longer anyway—stop your rotten attitudinizing in the trenches. Eros and Thanatos, German youth nonchalantly adorning himself for death—a fit subject for romantic sentimentality. Another hideous Puccini idea from German middle-class romanticism: beauty and death are twins. One more provincial cliché for Germany's downfall. The good Lord above who, according to Hegel, was guiding the whole of it, must be a strange soul, an out-and-out impresario on his divine throne. Disgusting small-town ham act—that's what world history is.

But abruptly I knew: he was right, he was exactly right. So the Reich was not that important to him either. And while evening rations were being distributed, while we felt around in the dark for bologna and beer and jam, I leaned over to him, chewing and remarking casually, "Tonight I'm cutting out. Want to come along?" I'd never been a good soldier, but I knew that it was not a good idea to make such border crossings alone. It had to be done in twos so you could help each other. Alone, you were lost. My trenchmate looked at me, grinning a little in disbelief; he'd put his helmet back on long ago. He asked in astonishment, "Man, just go across? To the Amis? Are you crazy?"

"Yes," I said, "tonight. If you want to, you can come."

The kid muttered something to himself that

could be interpreted either way; at the moment he seemed more interested in his bologna.

There are iron-clad rules in war, tactical rules that you can always depend on, and one of them is that even the worst barrage stops soon after midnight. Then they leave you alone until dawn. That's when the heroes sleep. When the illuminated dial of my watch showed three o'clock on the nose, I climbed out of my foxhole, silently gathered up my things, poked him with my foot, and whispered, "Let's go, come along."

And the other rose as in a dream—perhaps he had been asleep—and crawled after me. Strange, I thought, if you just poke them the right way and say, "Let's go," they'll follow you to the ends of the earth.

Slowly we worked our way like beasts of prey in a primeval forest, foot by foot to the edge of the canal. There was a bridge up ahead, a narrow, iron viaduct that had long since been blown up, and its black girders plunged into the water. From our side you could use them to let yourself down. In the dark you could see no more than one cracked pylon and a metal rail that had slipped out of place and must end somewhere under water. We needed only to wait and see. Now we hung by our arms like apes from the black, slippery girder, clinging tight to the sides and letting ourselves down hand over hand. "Now farewell, my lovely home"—wasn't that a tune I'd learned in school?

Suddenly I heard a splashing and crashing, I felt water, and I let go. I was standing in the canal up to my belt buckle but no deeper, water gurgling and rushing around me. My God, we're giving ourselves away. Anybody who's anywhere near can't help but hear us. We have been detected. All at once there was firing, a machine gun from our side, the brief bark of carbines. Then all was quiet again. It must have been a routine response on the part of the guards. So we stood in the water for a short eternity, not daring to move, trembling with cold and fear. My God, if they catch us now! We don't even have any ammunition left to return fire. But no, they won't catch me. I'd rather go down, drowning or tearing the weapon from their hands, pushing in their faces with the gun butt and shooting myself. You will not catch me alive, gentlemen. This is the end. I have decided. I'd rather be dead than go on being a German soldier. The bridge has collapsed, and I am already standing deep in the water, swimming westward. Now farewell—I'm joining the enemy.

The night after Easter at the Dortmund-Ems Canal. The water rose high and sometimes burped up bubbles from the tops of our boots. The Lord is risen; truly, He is risen. They shot Hermann, and now all of us would be shot; I did not want to go on, I could not go on. Once I was a soldier, once I was a student, once I was a son from Berlin whose parents had high hopes of him. Now in Berlin the morose man raged and allowed everything to be burned to the ground. In the end he would burn himself up. We had been caught in the gristmill of history, we children of the middle class from Hamburg and Breslau, we sons of Germany; now we would be ground up one by one, like a thousand grains of corn, threshed and stirred into the cake batter of history. Others were stirring the cake—the Americans and the Russians, the British and the French—and the Germans were being threshed. Thank God, the Germans were finished in history. I had abandoned my people. I was free.

And then, unexpectedly—barely an hour can have passed—we were actually standing on the other side, on the other shore. Our feet rested on enemy soil. I was twenty-five years old, dripping wet, trembling with cold and fear, and for the first time I stood on German soil free of Hitler. German soil free of Hitler? Look at it, look at this dark, grassy soil beneath your feet, drained by winter; look at them, these few square yards of Westphalian soil, enemy soil. Such a thing is possible: the soil on which you stand no longer belongs to him, no longer supports either SS or judge advocates. German soil free of Hitler, free Germany in the dark of the night—can there really be such a thing? Your whole youth has been redeemed; Germany can be wrested from him, it is really possible. Throw yourself to the ground, kiss the earth. Say, He is risen. Respond, Truly, He is risen.

We did not throw ourselves to the ground, we did not kiss the earth, but I know that I said to Jürgen, "Come on, throw it away now." And we took our carbines and our steel helmets, our side arms and our gas masks, and dropped them on the soil that was free of Hitler.

I was fourteen years old when Hitler came to power; all I ever knew was this Reich, his Reich, our Reich, all I ever knew was hatred and war and that all of us must sacrifice ourselves to the last. All I ever heard was that out there the Jews, the Bolsheviks, and the plutocrats ruled, all of them enemies, all of them aborigines, all of them subhuman creatures intent on destroying our poor, proud land. I had never seen an American or a Russian. Actually I had no idea who these people were whose side I was joining or what would be waiting for me there. I only knew, For the first time, here is Germany free from Hitler, here is soil he no longer rules. His power is broken. The earth is good.

No Easter greeting, then, no Easter thanks, but all the same something like a childish dance of joy: Jürgen, we made it! We are free, we are no longer soldiers, the war is over! Do you know what it means—the war is over? The war is like a black, poisonous cloud that comes over people, paralyzes them, blinds them; there's nothing you can do to stop it. But now we've done something to stop it, we've broken out of the circle of death, we've outfoxed the common fate. We couldn't prevent the war—of course we couldn't—but we could end it. We, and only we. That is our achievement, our deed. Tonight, on the night after Easter Sunday of 1945, the war between Germany and the world came to an end, and we two were the ones who had done it.

We were like two generals on their way to sign the surrender agreement. Our real generals were not about to do it; they were still fighting for Hitler. So we had to, Jürgen and I. Two privates first class would go to the enemy and say, "The Second World War is over." We would capitulate in the name of Germany. Our leaders weren't doing it, after all.

We had been walking for half an hour, simply crossing the fields, strolling like real civilians. We were sure we'd run across something any moment now, but we ran across nothing. Behind us, to the east, dawn was breaking. The Americans were apparently not prepared to sacrifice their soldiers in close combat. Their heavy guns had been deployed way at the rear, and in front of them there may have been a few sentries and grenade launchers—nothing more.

It was a damp, foggy March morning around five o'clock, no longer night but not yet day, the hour when you feel sickeningly hung over on guard duty, not quite asleep and not quite awake but both at the same time. My God, think of the many times you stood guard in Russia at five o'clock in the morning, waiting for the break of day with a disgusting taste in your mouth, thinking, How long can this business with Hitler go on? Nowhere in the world are sunrises more beautiful, more expansive, more fantastic than over Russia's plains. The colors flicker from reddish violet to pale yellow, staging a combat between light and dark, as in the desert. Yes, in the desert the sun may be just as large as it is over Russia. All that was long ago. The Germans had long since been driven from Russia, they had been driven from the desert, and now they were standing watch here. Here in Germany everything was small and narrow, dark and damp; here the sun rose and set without grandeur.

Suddenly I heard rattling and quick footsteps. "Stop, Jürgen," I said. "Don't move. Can't you hear? That's not the shrubbery." And just as suddenly a group emerged from the fog of dawn. I had never seen an American soldier before, and yet I knew at once. That's them—of course. They appeared out of the dark like ghosts and abruptly stood before us like poplars in the night, huge as giants, two black men and two white, in gray-green field uniforms, submachine guns cradled in their arms, grenades fastened to their belts, their helmets carelessly shoved back on their heads. So they were trotting off to the front.

When they became aware of us, they were galvanized by astonishment. "Oh, Germans!" one exclaimed, whistling through his teeth, and those behind him were already raising their arms in surrender, thinking they had fallen into the hands of a German patrol. They preferred to give themselves up—"Safety first." Both of us were wet and bareheaded. We were completely unarmed, and we had a hell of a time making it clear that we did not want to capture them but wanted them to capture us. It was so difficult to explain the cast of characters; it took some time.

My schoolboy English turned out to be exceedingly inadequate to such a task. It was true that I knew Shakespeare and a little Milton, I had studied English for nine years—but how actually to phrase this sort of thing, the business about Hermann Suhren, about our generals and Hitler and that there was to be peace now? I had not learned that part. I paraphrased, I fumbled my words, and I stuttered something or other. Gradually they understood, they nodded. One laughed briefly and scratched his neck reflectively, and after a while the leader said, "Okay." I did not know this word, I had never heard it before, but then the others surrounded us and said, "Go on, let's go," and set out with us. Now farewell, we are firmly in the enemy's hands. We made it.

For every stranger, America is a true miracle. When one morning the ship makes fast at the piers of Manhattan, a wide, bold, sensible, and fantastic world awaits the traveler. I had never seen it, and yet—my miracle was greater, my America more astonishing. I moved directly from Unna and Lünen to the States, I came straight from Hitler's Reich. It was like a jump cut in the cinema of time.

We found ourselves in a United States Army command post set up in an old farmhouse, but the surroundings were a strange mixture of tennis club and airplane instrument panel, with many soldiers, white and colored, many telephones and walkie-talkies. Some of the men wore headphones and at the same time listened to a portable radio that blared the sounds of jazz. All were neatly dressed and healthy, moved loosely and flexibly. They treated each other like members of an athletic team, and they all wore very tight trousers and gray-green shirts. I kept looking for shoulder patches, I couldn't tell the officers from the enlisted men. I stood there like a dummy, staring, watching them talk with each other—short and yet to the point; watching them smoke—casually and yet a little addicted; watching them phone—firmly and yet very relaxed. Many had smart smiles on their lips when they talked, and they never stopped smiling. Others were downright exuberant, like boys playing at cowboys and Indians. Did that mean they were having an exuberant war over here?

I did not know; everything was so confusing and strange to me. All I suddenly knew, before I'd said a single word, was how stale, horrible, and rancid was the world I have come from. On our side all military men parted their hair, had pimply faces, displayed pinched expressions, stood at attention before glittering shoulder bars. And they shouted. Everyone shouted in Germany; the Führer shouted at the provincial governors, the generals shouted at the officers, the officers shouted at the sergeants, and my corporal shouted at me: You asshole—and you claim to have a college education?

And now I stood here, Germany's most piteous son, a turncoat and traitor. My uniform, soiled and wet, dripped on the ground, my face was damp and mud-streaked, my hands were black with mud. I did not even have a cap anymore. I looked like a dog that's been out in the rain, a dog that's been pulled out of a ditch. And I heard myself say in an almost inaudible voice, "I came of my own free will. I brought Jürgen Lubahn from Lübeck with me. We hate this war. We hate Hitler. None of our fellow soldiers is anything more than a hospital case. If you'll stop your terrible weapons, gentlemen, I'll explain our positions, the little that I know. But you must stop this carnage. We don't have any more ammunition."

I really did say "gentlemen," and I made my whole speech in German, for after he had listened to some of my attempts at English, the uniformed man who was interrogating me—he seemed to be a lieutenant—said, "You may speak German. This is Corporal Levison. He studied in Heidelberg with Professor Alfred Weber and Professor Karl Jaspers. He will interpret."

I know it sounds absurd, but that's how it was. I had left the filth of trench warfare to join the enemy. I was a student of philosophy, and the first words I heard, the first names my enemy spoke to me, were Weber and Jaspers. The names of sociologists and philosophers had never been mentioned in my unit. There was no such thing as the mind as far as paratroopers were concerned. Theirs was the world of foot soldiers and mercenaries; they said "shit" and screwed up their faces, yelling and drinking beer all the while.

A long conversation ensued between Corporal Levison and me. I'll never forget it as long as I live, that miniature colloquium on the Monday after Easter of 1945, at seven o'clock in the morning. He said Heidelberg and I said Freiburg. He said Jaspers and I said Heidegger. "Before I was drafted," I said, "I studied in Freiburg with Heidegger. That interested him enormously. He was apparently a German Jew, one of those who were able to get out. He was now attached to the regiment as an interpreter and special adviser on Germany. He loved Germany and was extremely happy to have found someone in his chosen field among all those uniformed bodies, and he and I carried on a long discussion about Heidegger and Jaspers, their similarities and differences. We spoke of Dasein analysis, the mysticism of Being, and ontological distinctions, interrupted by reports from the front—the radio was still playing jazz—and then we discussed whether and to what extent Being could be extrapolated from Existence. At that point Heidegger had not yet undergone his conversion.

Everything seemed a little fantastic and dreamlike: I had abandoned my people and my homeland, and now I found them again, here in the enemy's command post. They knew all about the mind, they knew something about our philosophers and thinkers, and Corporal Levison's eyes shone at the mention of Heidelberg. He began to warn me about Heidegger, who represented a dark byway of Germany and was not to be compared with the breadth and brightness of Alfred Weber.

Jürgen Lubahn was still standing next to me

with his dark, wet mop of hair. Was he still carrying his mirror? Everything must be incomprehensible to him, must seem like a conspiracy. There stood the representatives of the American army, drinking instant coffee, smoking cigarettes. The officers were asking about our positions, and it was already daylight, but we spoke only of German philosophy and why Germany had come to such a dreadful end. Suddenly I thought, You see, what you sought is real. You were always looking for something and did not know if it existed. My God, how can that be? You lived in Germany for twenty-five years, four of them in the army, always kept silent, always accepted everything, never felt at home in Germany—and you haven't been with the enemy for more than an hour, and already you feel at home here. You are no longer alone in the world. The enemy—he is your world.

What happened next was very quick. The ice had been broken, and now the stream gushed forth. I reported to the Americans about our positions. I said, "They lie here and here, and there they have another grenade thrower, and further back there's an ackack battery. Of our hundred or so men, many still have carbines, but only a few have even two or three rounds of ammunition left. And there are no more heavy weapons at all. At the rear, everybody is starting to flee. So stop your heavy artillery."

It took barely twenty minutes for the noise to

actually cease in our sector of the front. Suddenly there was quiet, and I thought, That is your accomplishment, your Easter peace.

They stopped the artillery and assembled a fighting unit to go over as shock troops, and it couldn't have been more than ten o'clock or ten thirty when they came back with a huge catch, as if they'd been on an unexpectedly fruitful fishing trip. They brought our whole unit; they'd simply captured them. How am I ever to forget that moment? Uwe and Heinz, Fritz and Peter, you guys from Brandenburg and Berlin, from Munich and Hamburg—all of you were prisoners now. And I stood there, leaning against a jeep, smoking the cigarette they gave me: Lucky Strike, my thirty pieces of silver. I did betray them, of course; but then again, I did not betray them. I brought them out of this bloody Fortress Europe, I rescued them from the blood soup the morose man in Berlin was making of us all. The Germans were not worth his tragic sense after all.

They walked past me, silent and beaten, misled men; they walked like all the world's prisoners—tired, exhausted, dulled. They were not even aware that I was the cause of their imprisonment. They thought I was brought in a few minutes earlier. When you're part of the end of the world, who knows which is the first, which the last? They did not notice my flight, either. They would never find out that today, here at the Dortmund-Ems Canal, one of their fellow soldiers put an end to the war in a sector a scant kilometer wide. That wasn't a whole lot, one kilometer. All the same, it would remain my secret.

In the afternoon they shaped us up into a prisoner-of-war company. A sergeant came and said, "I want this man to step forward," and I was taken before Corporal Levison and the lieutenant one more time. Their unit was already on the move; they would strike camp now, would push farther into Germany by way of the Ruhr. From Unna to Hitler it would take them a bare four weeks. And the lieutenant said, "We are very grateful to you. You did well. But we cannot help you now. You will be imprisoned, you will be a prisoner like all the others. Do you understand?" After hesitating a while, he added, "Give me your paybook. At least I can make a notation in it. Perhaps it can be of use to you someday with our people." And he took the paybook, opened it to the first page, and under my number he wrote in pencil, in small script, four words that, when I read them left me slightly embarrassed and stunned. My God, what nonsense, I thought. But later it came to me, All the same, no German officer would ever have written that about you.

I hadn't quite left the command post yet when a black GI came over and said, "Hand over your

watch, give me your money. Hurry up, dammit."
In soldiers' slang that's called filching. I gave him
my watch and my money, and I knew once and for
all that now I was a regular prisoner of war, like
millions of other Germans.

The wonderful, incredible freedom of imprisonment now began. It inaugurated a period of
suffering infused with hope. I lived only in the
mass, in tired, dull, hungry heaps that were
shoved from camp to camp, from cage to cage. And
yet I came to life again for the first time in the
midst of this great gray army of the vanquished. I
felt, Now your time is coming. Now you will
awaken, now you will come to. With Hitler as the
victor, it never would have worked anyway. Now
we are way at the bottom, but this bottom holds
hope, has a future, offers opportunities. Things
are going badly for you, but you know that they
can get better, they will get better. For the first
time I felt what the future actually is: hope that
tomorrow will be better than today. A future—
there never could have been such a thing under
Hitler.

We had been brought to France, where we
were kept in the Cherbourg camp. Untold millions
were still falling into the hands of the Allies, who
were not prepared for the sudden, wild capitula-
tion of a great and humbled people. There was a lot
of hunger, misery, and rain. We stood in a meadow

like cattle, crowded close. I did not even have a coat anymore. We stood for days and nights on end—there are few things more horrible than standing all night in a wet meadow, and then another night. We walked up and down wrapped in jackets and blankets. Men were throwing away their medals and shoulder bars. The ground teemed with braid and iron crosses, and we stepped on them and on the old fifty-mark notes that lay among them. It was all worthless now anyhow, you heard people say, and if we ever got a cigarette, we took pleasure in lighting it with a ten-mark note twisted into a spill; it seemed a cheap and classy form of amusement.

A lot happened to us. One day in Cherbourg we were given a POW newspaper that announced in big letters, HITLER DEAD. He was alleged to have perished in the Battle for Berlin, and the paper even gave a list of new cabinet members, headed by Admiral of the Fleet Dönitz. Some of the men awoke from their lethargy, many did not believe the newspaper, most didn't care one way or another, but for me this was another occasion for astonishment.

I can still see myself lying in the big tent we had been given by this time. It was a beautiful, sunny May morning, very warm even so early in the day. The others were outside, sitting on rocks, waiting for chow, rolling something to smoke out of a kind of straw, brooding to themselves. And I was holding this piece of paper. I could not believe that there was such a thing: paper printed with words in the German language, a whole news-paper that wasn't made by Nazis. A real German newspaper without hatred and oaths of allegiance and the reaffirmation of eventual German victory. It was like a miracle: that the German language was possible even without Hitler, that it could exist against him, that such a thing could be done—German letters, German sentences against Hitler.

When I first began to read the newspapers, he was already in power. I knew nothing but a subser-vient, bellicose, boastful press. I always felt it was a proven fact that Hitler had also conquered and occupied the German language, and my parents had always told me, "What you read in the papers isn't true, but you musn't say so. Outside, you must always act as if you believe everything." The German language and lies had become one and the same thing to me. Home was the only place where you could speak the truth. What you read in the papers was always a lie, but you weren't allowed to say so. And now I was holding a newspaper that was in German and that did not lie. How was it possible? How could language and truth coincide? How did it happen that you could believe something you saw in print? It was the first free German paper of my life.

Only later did I take in what I had actually read. It was the following night. We were lying in our large tent on the bare ground of France, closely ranked. Nobody could turn over without pulling his neighbor with him; it was a complicated form of collective sleeping. I has awoken from confused dreams, and suddenly in the dark I saw the headline once more, huge in front of me, and I thought, You made it! You're actually living to see the day! He is really dead, and no knight of the Iron Cross will bring him back to life. Hitler is dead—did you hear that, you guys? His power is gone, he has departed this life. Like all creatures, he too must die; even Hitler is mortal. How does it happen that even the powerful must die? Haven't they conquered death? You never thought it was possible—tell the truth. You never dared to hope that he would die first; you always believed that he was the more powerful, the greater, the stronger.

Him or me—the equation had always come out in his favor. I knew as early as 1941 that he would not win; it was evident when he declared war on Russia and then on the United States that he could not possibly win. But I always had a somber conviction that he would succeed in dragging out his defeat for a long time, perhaps for an eternity. Europe was a fortress in those days, after all, and the Allies were slow to garner victories. He held all of us in his iron grip. All of us were his workers, his soldiers, his slaves, and his servants.

I was standing guard in Paris, at the gates of the Lariboisière Hospital, where one had such a surprising view of the white dome of Sacré-Coeur. It was Christmas 1941, cold and windy, and as snowflakes sweep across the boulevards, I thought, It will go on and on like this forever—winter and summer. He has conquered me, he has conquered us all. All of Europe lies at his feet. We live in bunkers and ditches for him, we throw up entrenchments, we fire guns for Hitler, all of Europe is a single barracks that he will garrison for tens of years. I will be thirty, forty years old; he has already stolen my youth, and he will steal my whole life; one day he will topple, but I will topple before he does. I no longer have the strength. The Continent is a camp for the Thirty Years' War of the Germans. That's how it is. It has happened before. I may hold on two or three years longer—no more. I will take my own life, I will prefer to shoot myself; I was simply born at the wrong time.

That's the way it is. I was born under Adolf Hitler. I had to start with that fact. No world, no century for me. Give myself up, let myself fall. Perhaps other parents in other ages would beget me anew. This was not my time. It was Hitler's time.

And now, suddenly, he was dead; the fortress was cracked and broken, the citadel stormed, the ring burst asunder, the demon wrestled to the ground. Hitler was dead, and I was alive. It was as if this were the night of my birth, happening for the first time. Now life would surely begin.

Further miracles began to follow daily. One morning an officer arrived, accompanied by two enlisted men carrying long lists. They started to sound us out, trying to identify Nazis and victims of Nazis, SS men and resistance fighters. We had to bare our chests, and it was during this examination that I learned for the first time that there were Germans who had their blood type tattooed on them as a sign of membership in the SS, and others who had numbers burned into the lower arm. The two groups were now separated, and there was a barbed-wire enclosure for those with the blood type and another camp for the people with the numbers above their wrists.

The SS camp remained half-empty; even in those days no one would admit to having taken part. It abutted directly on our camp, and in the evenings I could see them sitting there on rocks. They were thin, resigned men who sat staring at the ground, grim and stubborn, perhaps still hoping for a miraculous turn of events. They had lost the game. They had survived. It was not part of their world order to survive Hitler. Now they had to pay. Sometimes one of our guards walked over and spat at them, and the others—those with the numbers—now received little privileges, got more to smoke, and were given jobs. Surely they would be released sooner.

The sensation I felt was not revenge or triumph. All of us were prisoners, after all, German prisoners, a vanquished people; all of us were eating the same bitter gruel of defeat. But the idea that the defeat could restore justice was another incomprehensible realization. I stood at the door of our cage, surrounded by wood and barbed wire; other cages encircled our cage, other camps adjoined our camp. As far as I could see, nothing but rocks, wire, and wooden partitions, and behind each there were always more cages, with watchtowers at the corners. The world was a camp of human beings squatting behind barbed wire.

New transports arrived daily, plodding past me along the wide, graveled camp street like huge, weary herds. They had started to sort the ranks by now; since the previous day, all the arrivals were officers. They came in endless caravans, thousands of officers trudging by slowly like a gray, viscous mass. They were still wearing their shoulder patches, they still looked well-nourished; they came in rows of five, with dull downcast eyes, in ccats of field-gray and green and blue, and some had fat stomachs. Beside them walked the colorful guards driving them along energetically, like sheepdogs barking, "Go on! Let's go!" Sometimes they hit out when the endless procession came close to a standstill, bringing their little whips down on someone's back with a smack.

Germany, here are your grand masters, here is an end to your grandeur. A thousand officers are led to the trough like tired cattle—defeated leadership, yesterday's elite. Sometimes the faces looked like the aristocratic pride of Pomerania and Brandenburg, sons of Prussian noblemen who swore by the morose man in Berlin. The Americans were burying them now, blacks are herding them into large cages like wild animals. But they lost their honor before this, the airforce major and the army captain.

Now men with golden shoulder braid plodded past—they had to be officers of the rank of general; among them were others with red stripes along their trousers—members of the General Staff; and somewhere among them I bet there was the paratroop lieutenant who shot down Hermann Suhren—he had lost his honor before now. And all of them, dusty and ragged and almost drugged, shuffled in rows of five into large cages. That was how a wild nation was led into captivity.

I stood behind my fence and reflected that the image was not new. For millennia nations had been conquered and armies vanquished this way, and the victor always claimed the right to transfigure his victory into a victory of the good, his triumph into the triumph of justice. That was the sublime lie of world history, the right of the mightier. It had never been true. We knew.

This one time it really was true: our guards represented the good, and the men out there stood for evil. Now, in our cracked and broken Fortress Europe, the penitentiaries and prisons, the camps and death factories were thrown open, the sacrificial victims were saved, the dead were honored, the oppressors were punished. There had never been anything like it in the world. Look at it, hold on to it, never forget it as long as you live. Once there was a war which the Germans and Hitler lost, and their defeat restored the world order. Good was triumphant, and evil was vanquished. Justice ruled the world. It was almost like the Last Judgment: the mills of death stood still, the sheep were separated from the goats, the persecutors and the persecuted were differentiated, a great book was opened.

And I thought, So you survived Hitler. Someday you will be released from Cherbourg. You will begin to live, you will learn, you will work, have a career, grow older, and gradually you will forget your youth under Hitler. But not this, this one hour in Cherbourg, when justice triumphed. You saw with your own eyes that such a thing is possible. Repeat it to the others; it has been promised us for so long. The dream of nations—justice. One thousand nine hundred and forty-five years after Christ. Once there was a year when the history of mankind almost became Judgment Day for mankind.

Day of Judgment

Last night's dream: I am standing in a barracks yard. I am still in the army, but now it is called Federal Armed Forces. Everyone is wearing a new, cheerful uniform, bright and attractive; I am the only one still wearing my old, tattered airforce togs from the Russian campaign—ragged blue-gray, crumpled, faded, spots on the coat, my private-first-class stripe wavy with shabbiness. I intend to get a new outfit in the clothing room, but I am not given one. I have annoyed the orderly by addressing him as "sergeant, sir." "You ass," he shouts back, "can't you see that I'm a master sergeant?" Oh, yes, I must have made a mistake about his stripes.

I remembered the dream now, as I drove through Berliner Strasse—of course, last night I dreamed about the army; the war was on again. Berliner Strasse runs through downtown Frankfurt, parallel to the river. It was built after the war, which destroyed the old part of the city, and it was designed to relieve traffic congestion. Like so many other items of our modern city planning, it was only half a success. Even before traffic gets to Saint Paul's Church, it is backed up.

I sat in my car. It was Thursday, February 27, 1964, one of those wonderful, clear, sunny days you get before it is really spring, when you should take off for the country, the mountains. A seductive day, bright, light blue and silver. Around noon, it would grow warm. I had pushed the roof all the way back, and I tried in vain to light a cigar while I drove. I was thinking about my dream— what was the point of it? It was not true, after all. I was no longer the enlisted man in his old uniform. Hitler was dead. My youth was past. The dream, then, was false.

All the people in this country wore new things—sixty million Germans in new clothes, and I was one of them. This city seemed entirely made up of the new: banks and department stores, display windows and cars sent out the cold, handsome glow of industrial artifacts. A new era had begun, the era of universal technical civilization. Germany was an industrial giant in world civilization, and Frankfurt was its commercial center: prosaic and harsh, beautiful and brutal, a mixture of old Sachsenhausen and mini-Chicago.

I was on my way to the Auschwitz trials. We had read about them in the papers: accounts, eyewitness reports, commentaries. At first they aroused some attention, but soon they became occasions for indifference. Later, displeasure and satiety set in. What's the point? Everything was so complicated and so boring. Five years' preliminary investigation, we were told, and an indictment that ran to seven thousand pages—who could take in, understand, follow all that? It was a matter for specialists. It was like a topical play staged ten years too late, dated even as it opened. A serial novel that dragged on tenaciously for months, a story of horror that produced boredom among the public.

Concentration-camp atrocities—who could still listen to them, who could still be interested in them? We knew it all already. Obligatory coverage by the major papers, obligatory reading matter for no one, not proper material for the tabloids, not a suitable topic for cocktail parties. When I had said in passing, "I'm going to attend the Auschwitz trials," for a moment the evening's guests were stricken with embarrassment; an awkward hush ensued. "Yes, yes, terrible," someone at the back finally muttered. "You poor thing," a lady added, and the hostess poured more whiskey and tried to change the subject. I fell silent. There were no Nazis here; I had simply said the wrong thing at a party. In our country you did not deliberately say *Auschwitz*; the word was taboo.

I was driving to the Auschwitz trials because I

wanted to see for myself. I mean, seeing with your own eyes was supposed to exorcise the ghosts, and Auschwitz was like a ghost. The word had become a strange metaphor—the metaphor for evil in our time. Blood and fear and horror resonated in it— flayed, burned human flesh, smoking chimneys, and innumerable German bookkeepers zealously making note of everything. Auschwitz was like a new stanza in a medieval dance of death; we were reminded of bones and skeletons, of Death, the Great Reaper, of shrouds, and of the new mechanics of murder—gas.

They say that in our enlightened age there are no more myths; but always when I heard *Auschwitz* I felt as if a mythical avatar of death in our time were touching me—the dance of death in the industrial age, the new myth of managed death, which began there. Doesn't history give birth to new myths from time to time? Was Auschwitz not really Rosenberg's vision—the myth of the twentieth century?

I was driving to the Auschwitz trials to clarify the myth in me. I just wanted to sit there and listen, look, observe. It was my last chance. The wave of political trials had begun once again. It was important. It was our last opportunity to meet the past face to face, to see history in its actors, the doers and their victims, not as monuments of horror and suffering, but as people like you and me. I wanted to see this drama of my contemporaries before it toppled into the abyss of history. I wanted to have one more encounter with my youth under Hitler.

After this wave of trials the curtain of time would drop forever. The play would be finished. The material would become history, would be transferred to the hands of the historians. There would be dissertations, analyses, and scholarly interpretations. Children would learn about it in school grudgingly, as if it were an old poem to be memorized, stuff you have to know to get into the university, like the Pythagorean theorem or Xenophon's *Anabasis*. The word, Auschwitz, would have no more reality than Waterloo.

On this brilliant February day the Auschwitz trials were still being conducted in the aldermanic chambers of the Römer in Frankfurt. Frankfurt was a loud, busy, affluent city, a little feverish and vulgar, lots of Opel cars, lots of businessmen, but the ground here was imbued with the awesome consecration of history. Starting in 1562, all German emperors were crowned here. Only a few hundred yards away rose the Imperial Cathedral, which was not a cathedral at all since it was never an episcopal see, and which in fact was quite humbly the parish church of Saint Bartholomew. But once—who here knows?—these few hundred yards were the holy center of the Holy Roman Empire of

194

the Germanic Nation. The coronation logs described the solemn preparations made to receive the chosen one at the cathedral portals. They reported the coronation mass, the investiture with the imperial robes, the girding on of Charlemagne's sword. They told of the presentation of the national insignia, the proclamation and enthronement of the newly crowned head. Then a solemn train proceeded to the Church of Saint Nicholas and to the Römer, where the emperor, in full regalia, marched to his coronation feast, and the exercise of the hereditary offices began. Hallowed ground, where today Volkswagens and Opels, old Borgward limousines and new Mercedes hotly contested for position. Thus history ended in parking lots.

A little old man, a pensioner type, used his unsteady hand to direct the cars, which threatened to become stuck in the soft mud. He took it upon himself to play at parking attendant. For this huge mud complex between the cathedral and the Römer was not a real parking lot; it was only a large, empty embarrassment of the 1960s confronting the forces of history. What was to be built here? In 1792, three years after the French Revolution broke out, on the very spot where I was now driving around and around in circles searching in vain for a parking space, the last emperor of the Holy Roman Empire was anointed. It was the

195

Hapsburg Francis II, and the coronation took place—irony of history—on July 14, Bastille Day. Today was February 27, 1964, and inside the Römer there was a trial about Auschwitz. This was the twentieth day of the proceedings.

I was a little dizzy as I went up the steps to the Römer. It was not Auschwitz that frightened me; it was justice. Always I felt some anxiety when faced with German prosecutors, judges, and policemen. I had a recurring nightmare that I was standing at the bar of German justice once again, as I did in 1941: People's Tribunal, Berlin, third floor, criminal proceedings against Broghammer and others. And among these "others" I too was once included, in a preliminary investigation— "Preliminaries Concerning an Action for High Treason." The place was swathed in crimson flags, and a powerful national eagle dominated the center of the hall; three lawyers and nine lay judges, SS and Party, and in front of them, in the seats reserved for the audience, prominent political and military figures. Silence, chill, fear in the room.

Those were German judges who, in the name of the people, pronounced sentence—German judicial officials and German policemen—and since that time it was difficult for me to tolerate their harsh, responsible faces, German visored caps, prognathous jaws, the very limited physiognomy of administrative competence. I was always a little afraid of the uniforms. I knew I was wrong and should struggle against this feeling; we lived in a new, a better state. But now, as I passed the group of green policemen, I felt it again. Now something really ought to happen. Now one of the men in uniform should step forward and say, "You, the accused—come with me. The court has already convened." But none of them moved. I was no longer the accused—for the first time.

I showed my press card and another paper from the court, and I heard myself saying, like a stranger, "I am a German journalist, and I am here to attend the Auschwitz trials." The three men in green cast a cursory glance at my papers, touched the visors of their caps, and then said politely, "Yes, please, this way, three flights up, please." They made room for me so I could enter the reception hall.

Down here someone was just getting married. The Römer in Frankfurt is an age-old setting for marriages. It is where the municipal offices are located, and it is a venerable, famous, and popular site for young couples. They were allowed to ascend the narrow, handsome imperial staircase—built in 1752, and a source of delight to Goethe in his youth—to get to the wedding chamber. Even today, while the criminal case against Mulka and others was being tried upstairs, marriages were being performed two flights down. Young people in festive clothing sat on the benches waiting to be called. A wallboard displayed the latest banns. Witnesses and family members stood around awkwardly. In one corner a photographer was kneeling in front of two newlyweds and said, "Say cheese." The bride, in her white dress and veil, holding a huge bouquet of roses, produced a cramped smile. It was going to be one of many family photographs, mawkish, saccharine, and a little stiff, that would later stand on a German sideboard in a faded silver frame; and in twenty years this amiable young man in a tuxedo, who was now smiling shyly at his bride, would surely be a resigned, pinched German civil servant, a little pedantic and musty, and perhaps he would hate this woman and she would hate him. And that would be a marriage, quite a normal, proper marriage.

The photographer had just set off his flash. For a fraction of a second the couple stood in the brilliant flood of light as if they were on stage. On the back of the wedding picture the date would be inscribed—Frankfurt, February 27, 1964—and they would not know that on this very Thursday, in this very building two floors up, a Viennese physician raised his hand to take the oath and swore to the truth of the statement "Two point nine to three million people, according to our calculations, were killed in Auschwitz." And he added, "So help me God." Downstairs the marrying went on, more rings were exchanged, more kisses were bestowed, more photographs were snapped for the family album twenty years hence. Was that our life?

I had been sitting in this aldermanic chamber for an hour. After some confusion, a policeman had brought me through a side door guarded by four officials and had snuck me into the last rows for spectators. The trial had been under way for some time. I had come late—because there was no adequate parking.

As always happens when you arrive at a movie or play after it has started, I sat there a little perplexed and benumbed and could not find my place in the plot. I sat there and thought, So this is it, this is the famous Auschwitz trial, and I distinctly felt a little disappointment rising in me. I had thought it would be different, harsher, more dignified, more dramatic—the prosecution in tall chairs, and the accused, abased on low benches. I remembered the Nuremberg trials and all the television coverage of the Eichmann trial—the man in the glass booth. Those proceedings had an element of stature and drama: Day of Judgment, nemesis, the tribunal and verdict of history. Where was it here?

I found myself seated in a medium-sized, pleasantly middle-class hall in which a board of inquiry was clearly in session. The room was about a hundred and twenty yards long and forty yards wide, with walls paneled in wood all the way up to the ceiling—pale brown, cheap wood. Green draperies concealed a stage to the right, with a large relief map representing the camp of Auschwitz mounted next to it. Eight lamps reminiscent of the stiff modernism of the 1930s lit the high-ceilinged room. On the main wall hung the blue, red, and white coats of arms of the nation and the city.

The hall, the solid administrative furniture— slightly clumsy benches and lighter, modern chairs— and even the faces of the judges seated under the coats of arms radiated solid middle-class spirit, respectable calm and paternalism. A serious and circumspect enterprise, surely fit for worthy city fathers. The presiding officer was a short, stocky, round-headed gentlemen perhaps in his late fifties. He sat behind huge piles of documents, and sometimes he turned a page or two. To the right and left of him sat the other two judges, one of them young, the other very old; they too turned the pages of documents. A voice came over the loudspeaker.

I looked around the hall for the defendants, but I could not find them. I looked for the witness stand, but I could not locate it. I had a good seat, I could see everything, but it all seemed so strange, so incomprehensible and confused. There were about a hundred and twenty or a hundred and thirty Germans in this chamber, citizens of our nation, Federal Republican Germans of the year 1964, and I could not tell who here actually were the accusers and who the accused.

Over the loudspeaker the voice, somewhat dusky and blurred, cut through the room. It must be the voice of the witness, and since I could not yet identify the roles being acted out here, I decided simply to listen. The voice said, "Birkenau was divided into three parts, B I, B II, and B III." After a pause it continued. "And then there was the mysterious B IIb Division, a mystery in this hell, a segment of Auschwitz where women and children and men lived together, did not have their heads shaved. The children were even given milk and had a nursery school." After another pause the voice added, "But the bitter end came for them as well. Six months after their arrival, the more than three thousand residents of B IIb were suddenly gassed."

A few moments later the voice rang from the loudspeaker again. "I will now describe my own arrival in Auschwitz. I was first sent to Auschwitz I, to the original installation. Even before we arrived at the camp, the SS people came up to us and asked, 'Do you have any money? A watch? Give it here. You won't be able to hold on to it in the camp anyhow. I'll help you out in the camp.' Over the gate through which they marched us was written, Work Liberates. There was waltz music to the left, a band was practicing. It never occurred to us that we were going to be sent to hell. Everything looked so peaceful, so calm."

The voice broke off again. The large chamber was very quiet now. A woman in one of the front rows had begun to weep. The voice told how they had been brought to the washroom, how they stood there naked, crowded close, and did not know whether water or gas would come out. "We waited and waited, but nothing happened. The only thing we could do was to lick at the dripping water. At night we were driven outside, into the open air—it was a cold night in May, there was a soft drizzle of rain—and we stood and waited, we stood all night long. The following morning we were shaved, but you can hardly call it shaving; they pulled out our hair. And then we were told, 'You will now be given your clothing number, and you have to remember it; it is important for your release.' But it was only the number that was tattooed into our skin. Then we realized clearly that we were not people, only numbers now."

The voice from the loudspeaker faltered. The sentences had grown slower and more hesitant. The pauses lengthened, their silence audible in the chamber—pauses of remembrance for the speaker, pauses of embarrassment for the audience. It was as if everyone were staring into space; stricken and rigid, everyone gazed straight ahead. Some women held handkerchiefs to their faces as the voice resumed. "I could already see the chimneys. I was standing at the doors of the gas chamber when my detail was suddenly led away from the crematorium. Everything seemed puzzling. We learned the truth only afterward. The corpses of a transport from France, which had been gassed during the night and had not yet been carted off, prevented the assassination of still more victims. And then, later, another miracle happened. An SS man came and asked, 'Are you a doctor? Are you a good doctor?' I said, 'I don't know.' He took me away, and that was how I was saved. After that, I was made a doctor in the quarantine section, and it was not until then that I discovered the purpose of the camp."

And the voice went on telling how the man slowly learned his way around the camp, settled in, and learned to live with the machinery of death. To have lived in Auschwitz for five years—to have survived Auschwitz—meant not only to have suffered for five years but also to have become accustomed to it, to have made one's peace with it, to have come to terms with it, with indifference, coldness, even one's own wickedness in the face of the misery of the lost.

Horrifying confirmation: man is the product of his environment. In the city of death, everyone becomes a supporting player. Whether you hand

203

out bread or gas, you are part of it. Only those who go along with the mechanics of annihilation have a chance of surviving. An incomprehensible, raging will to survive must have ruled the man with the voice—I won't die, not me, I will survive. Greed and desperation—only to remain, only to win through, to cling to one's piece of bread. To eat, to drink, to obey, to work, to participate, not to go under, to endure—to endure in order to bear witness some day to what man did to man in this place. The time would come; it would take twenty years, it would be February 27, 1964, it would be in Frankfurt. Now the hour, the absurd delusion and fantasy from Auschwitz, was here. The hour of truth had arrived.

A strange excitement took hold of me. For the last two hours I had been sitting in the Römer unable to find my place. It was as if the grid of history had been jumbled up. What time was it here and now? The time of those days? It was wartime, it was 1943; everything was as it was in those days. Winter in the East, war in Poland and Russia. I was twenty-two years old again. I was in Vitebsk, in Orel, in Smolensk, among cathedrals riddled with bullets and Party headquarters cracked and broken in the inner city, among the small, straw-roofed huts of the Russians closer to the outskirts. There were no more men; they were dead or captured or in Stalin's armies. Only women in rags—rags covering their bodies and their heads, their feet wrapped in wide, tattered rags—women who tried to trade in precious salt or little bits of cornbread hard as stone. I was only a private first class driving a truck, an Opel, but to these careworn, ragged Russian women I was one of the powerful victors, one of the green angels of death, inspiring universal fear.

It was a winter of war in Russia, a cold, bleak day in the snow-covered steppes, the ground frozen hard as marble, creaking under my snow chains. I was driving from the base to the front, past endless white forests; you could drive for hours in this huge land without advancing by so much as a step. Was Russia endless? Was Russia the world? The motor hummed brightly in second gear. I was carrying a load of soldiers, German paratroopers—twenty young, healthy, harmless men with machine guns and carbines. Sometimes, when we drove through potholes and the truck rumbled and swung clumsily up and down, they swore. I was taking a detachment of paratroopers to the front—a front intended to shield not only Berlin but also Auschwitz. I came from Berlin, but I had never heard the name Auschwitz.

The witness had just used the word *Sanka*. I was startled. Surely I was familiar with that term? Was it the name of a place in the East, a medication? Surely I'd heard it before? It was so difficult to remember everything after twenty years. While I was still trying to puzzle out this strange, foreign-sounding word, I heard the voice saying, "Most of them were hosed down with phenol in the *Sankas*," and suddenly the meaning appeared; from the shafts of the past it rose. Memory of my youth, memory of the technical language of ordnance and battalions, the hated, horrible language of the military, of which I was a part. *Sanka* was short for *Sanitätskraftwagen*, an ambulance, and in those days I, in the Second Company of the First Paratroop Regiment, drove one. Of course. They were the small, maneuverable white busses with the red cross on the roof, and they were also made by Opel. The *Sankas* were used to cart off the wounded, and sometimes the passengers cried and moaned and wished their driver to hell. I drove my *Sanka* to the central field dressing station in Smolensk. I was simply following orders, like seventy million other Germans. All of us were simply following orders.

But what would have happened if my travel orders had accidentally borne not the word *Smolensk* but that other word—the unknown, meaningless *Auschwitz*? How would it have been? Of course I would have taken my wounded there as well; of course—a soldier always does as he is ordered. I would have taken them to Auschwitz, and perhaps I would have delivered them to the very prison doctor who was now bearing witness. One or two wounded a day for the medical barracks in Auschwitz—that wasn't a lot.

And then? What else would I have done? It could hardly have escaped my notice that the business there was not curing but killing. What would I have done? Probably, like all the others, I would have closed my eyes, and for a while I would have acted as if I hadn't noticed a thing. Perhaps I would have hated my staff sergeant and my platoon leader even more, I would have clenched my fist in my coat pocket, and in the evenings I would have listened to the BBC. But what else?

I did not volunteer for the paratroops; I was detached from the air force. And if they had detached me to Auschwitz? After all, in that chaotic, confused time, anything was possible. Why not transfer a private first class who was no good for anything at the front to a work camp at the rear?

What would I have done? Would I really have been a hero? Would I really have stepped up to my lieutenant and said, "No, I won't do that. Not me. I refuse this order." After all, I would have gone there as a soldier, as a man in uniform, and I would have had a chance at survival—and my God, how I wanted to survive.

I think I would not have joined in the murdering, would not have been able to participate in the killing, the burning, the sorting out. That was another dimension. But wouldn't I have tried to somehow retreat from the affair into all the little subterfuges of a soldier's life? It is certain that I would not have been a hero. I would have withdrawn and kept my mouth shut—but who can say for how long? Even killing can become a habit. Everything is habit. If ten thousand people were killed each day, who is to say that after two years I wouldn't have become accustomed to that as well?

Someone must have opened the window of the chamber. From outside, street noises rose—noontime traffic in Frankfurt. A streetcar rumbled by. It was the 18 Line, which has a stop here between the Römer and Saint Paul's. I heard the conductor's bell ringing, the opening and slamming of the doors, the motor's bright hum, and then the rattle of the car through the street. The sound was helpful at this moment. The tram going by outside was a certainty. There was, after all, such a thing: genuine, everyday reality; people who now, at noon, rode from Praunheim to Riederwald and thought of everything except Auschwitz; women with shopping bags and men with black briefcases.

The squeaking and humming of the streetcar mingled strangely with the voice from the loudspeaker, which now spoke of children who, because the gas was scarce, were thrown alive into the fire. "There is no other way to make our quota," the directive from above had read. And they wanted to make their quota—of course. I felt fear and horror rising in me. Outside the 18 Line was rolling past, and here, inside, the Day of Judgment was happening. And I—where was I? Where did I stand?

I came as a stranger, a German journalist; all I wanted was to be a spectator. But as I followed the voice again, I felt that no one could remain a spectator here. The barriers of time had shifted out of place, past had become present, the cinema of life had been reeled backward and started again with a jerk. And why shouldn't this movie show us a scene that included me among many men in uniform, me in the campaign against the East? What would I be doing in this scene? Who would I be?

"We will recess for ten minutes." I must have been a little distracted, for the sentence came at me as if it had been delayed, and I saw everyone suddenly rising and moving toward the exits to the right and the left. I too rose, like a sleepwalker. I walked absently toward the door on the left, through which everyone was now pushing, and then I stood outside in the foyer and had no idea what to do.

The scene here was like intermission in a theater. The members of the audience got a breath of air, lit up cigarettes, stood around in groups, and critically discussed their impressions. A few of the gentlemen went to the checkroom and asked the attendant for their coats. Were they the ones who had been disappointed, who were dissatisfied—connoisseurs of the tragedy, abandoning the play in mid-performance?

Two older men in black silk robes—they must have been attorneys—were just coming from the men's room. One stopped at the mirror and gingerly, with a touch of vanity, tugged at his white tie; the other went to the checkroom attendant, laid down a few coins, and asked for a Coca-Cola. Then both returned to the foyer. The one with the Coke bottle must have told a joke, for the other abruptly burst into uncontrollable laughter: broad, portly Frankfurt citizens' faces, hearty laughter as in Sachsenhausen, joyous with wine and love of life. The everyday life of the attorney—why shouldn't a lawyer laugh on his time off?

Then someone spoke to me. It was a fellow reporter I'd known for years, a journalist from Hamburg. He spent time in a concentration camp himself, and now he started telling me. He had been here from the first day and knew everything; every night he telephoned his report to his radio station in Hamburg. He carried countless papers and notes, and he spoke of the assessors, lawyers, and defendants familiarly, as a theater critic might mention old, well-known actors. "And the defendants?" I asked eagerly. "Where are they, anyway?"

My colleague looked at me in astonishment.

He smiled ironically, put his hand to his mouth as if he were about to whisper, and answered, "Hey, man, can't you see? Right here, right next to you, back there. Those men in the armchairs, and those over there by the window, and the one at the checkroom counter. All over."

Then, for the first time, I understood that all these amiable people in the chamber, whom I took to be journalists or lawyers or spectators, that they were the defendants, and that of course there was no way to tell them from the rest of us. Twenty-two men stood accused here, eight were in prison, fourteen were free on bail, and with very few exceptions they all, of course, looked like everyone else, behaved like everyone else. They were well-nourished, well-dressed gentlemen of mature years—academicians, physicians, businessmen, manual laborers, caretakers—citizens of our affluent new German society. They were free Federal Republican citizens. Like me, they had parked their cars outside the building. They had come to the trial just like me. There was nothing to distinguish them. Suddenly I was reminded of a movie I'd seen shortly after the end of the war. It was called *The Murderers Are Among Us*. That was seventeen years ago.

Now an entirely new interest was roused in me. I was here again, back alive. I wanted to see them, recognize them, observe them. There must be something to differentiate them. Surely it must trouble them, set them apart, isolate them. It cannot be possible to prance around here bearing the burden of Auschwitz on your shoulders as if you were at the intermission of a play. Cautiously I approached the large leather couch along the wall. Five corpulent, good-natured gentlemen were sitting there, somewhat bulky and swollen, drinking Coca-Cola, smoking cigarettes, and chatting among themselves. Gentlemen during the break in a meeting of a corporate board of directors. Two of them seemed to be handicapped; they used black canes with rubber tips. They must have lived through a thing or two. The oldest of them, wearing a flawlessly cut navy-blue suit, had a slightly red face, and his hair was snow-white. My colleague said, "That's Mulka, Robert Mulka, SS Obersturmbannführer and aide to Höss, the camp commander. Today he's an exporter in Hamburg. He is staying at the Frankfurter Hof, the best hotel here, and on the days when the trial is in recess he jets to Hamburg to keep an eye on his business. The indictment accuses him, among other things, of having been responsible for the organization and security of the gassing equipment and for procuring the Cyclon B necessary for the gassing. Also collaboration in the sorting procedures at the loading platform and collaboration in the transport of the condemned to the gas chambers in trucks."

And I stood frozen, speechless, stealing glances at the man and quickly looking away again. I did not want to intrude, did not want to stare at the group the way you stare at strange wild animals in the zoo. I was aghast to find that murderers look like this—so harmless, so amiable and fatherly. But then I realized that these good-natured gentlemen were not the usual kind of murderers, not people who commit crimes of passion, who kill someone in a fit of temper or out of lust or desperation. All those are human motives. There are such things. But the men here were the modern murderers, a breed unknown until now, the administrators and bureaucrats of mass death, the bookkeepers and button pushers and clerks of the machinery, technicians who operate without hatred or feeling, small functionaries from the great realm of Eichmann—desk-chair murderers. Here a new style of crime became manifest: death as administrative action. These murderers were pleasant and proper civil servants.

Slowly the chamber began to fill up. The man in green at the entrance made a discreet sign to the spectators in the foyer. Those who had just been circulating, chatting together and smoking as at a party or at the Book Fair, broke apart, resumed their roles. Suddenly they formed a separate, isolated group, a political party continuing to play its judicial role. Court officials always have dramatic talent.

All at once I understood the seating arrangements in the chamber. The defendants were just in front of me: four rows, each row six seats wide, reaching down to the judges' bench. The eight prisoners came in from the right, accompanied by two policemen in blue. A prisoner with a brutal smile on his lips leaned down to his lawyer and spoke with him a while.

The fourteen defendants still at liberty had also taken their places; each one had two lawyers who sat to his right and spread out fat yellow file folders on the tables. Black block letters on them read "File Number 4 Ks 2/63," followed in parentheses by "In the Matter of Auschwitz." It moved me strangely to encounter such a code on legal folders again. And the parentheses, and the use of the word *Matter*.

Some things in the chamber were clearer to me now. The gentleman directly in front of me— earlier I had touched him on the shoulder to ask him about the defendants, but he did not answer— he was Schlage, Bruno Schlage, Defendant Number 8, caretaker and foreman bricklayer, with a simple, somewhat primitive face, thin hair worn in a crew cut, and the pinched features of German subordi-

214

nate types. The indictment accused him of having participated in the so-called bunker evacuations—that is, of having fetched the prisoners from their cells to be shot at the so-called black wall. "The accused is alleged to have participated in these shootings."

Directly in front of him sat a man who seemed interesting and intelligent. His name was Breitwieser, and he was a lawyer and legal adviser assigned to Auschwitz from 1940 on. He was Defendant Number 13. He seemed so likable and calm that I would hire him any day of the week. The indictment accused him of having "introduced the poison gas Cyclon B into the subterranean vaults, whereby about 850 Soviet prisoners of war and about 220 prisoners from the hospital were killed." Well over a thousand corpses, but that was more or less insignificant in this trial, and perhaps the defendant thought, They were only Russians, not Jews—isn't that right? Today he worked as a bookkeeper.

I leafed through the printed material my colleague from Hamburg handed me, and since the court had not yet been called into session, I quickly looked over what it said about Defendant Boger. Wilhelm Boger, born 1906 in Stuttgart. He sat at the front, assigned number 3; he was a commercial employee, also a bookkeeper. What did that mean? I thought. Was the SS made up entirely of bookkeepers? I always thought they were heroes, great warriors, Germanic men. I ran my eyes over what it said about selection, sorting out, gassing, mass shooting, the "black wall." All these were crimes involving untold numbers—mass murder, incomprehensible and anonymous. Basically they represented little that was new in the Boger case.

But then I read, "Furthermore, Boger is responsible for many individual actions. Thus, among others, he is charged with having killed Prisoner Secretary Tofler in Block 11 with two pistol shots; having held a sixty-year-old minister underwater in the prison kitchen until he was dead; having used a pistol to shoot and kill a Polish married couple with three children at a distance of about three yards; having kicked to death the Polish General Dlugiszewski, who had been starved until he was nothing but skin and bones; in the autumn of 1944, after the revolt of the special commandos had been put down, having joined other members of the SS in killing by pistol bullets in the back of the head about a hundred prisoners, who were ordered to lie on the ground in front of the crematorium."

I went on turning pages until I read, "Without reporting to the police, after the war Boger spent several years in the vicinity of Crailsheim, where he worked for farmers. Later he was employed in a commercial firm in Stuttgart." Again I thought, So he too was one—a decent, reliable bookkeeper, the kind they need in Stuttgart, a man you can depend on, a man who has adjusted, who can sleep at night and surely has buddies and friends and a family—the dead do not enter his dreams.

But right here in Hessen, in red Hessen, wasn't there a brave and courageous man, Chief State Counselor Bauer, a stroke of luck in our judicial system, a miracle in our land of civil servants? If Bauer had not insisted years ago, "We will have this trial whether it's popular or not; we'll hold it here in Frankfurt," then Boger might still be sitting faithfully behind his commercial lists in Stuttgart, drawing lines and dashes and sums in red, blue, and green, still not visited by his victims in his dreams.

And Mulka—intelligent, cultured, older, one-time aide to Höss and successful citizen of the republic—he would have continued to make his coffee-import deals from Hamburg, would be on good terms with foreign countries, would surely be a democrat kindly disposed toward the Christian Democratic Union but not active, obsequious toward the West, harsh toward the East. When he heard of brutality—and one heard such a lot about the brutality practiced in the East—he would always think of the Communists, of Bautzen, Waldheim, and Hilde Benjamin, and never of himself.

How was it possible after Auschwitz to become such a servile and accomplished citizen of the republic? How did one do it? What did the doctors, the psychologists, and the psychiatrists have to say about it? None of the defendants had become "conspicuous" again. All had managed to reestablish their lives, their homes, their positions, all were once again deserving and respected citizens of their communities, capable and successful, often well liked.

There at the front sat Kaduk, Defendant Number 10, Oswald Kaduk, butcher and male nurse by trade. His was one of the few repellent faces here. He must have been what our nightmares conjure up as the image of the concentration camp bully: always brutal, often drunk. The indictment accused him of thousands of killings, but here too the small, private bestialities that happened, as it were, in passing and after working hours seemed to me much more revealing: throttling, beating to death, maltreatment, throwing prisoners up against the barbed wire, whipping a condemned man because the noose broke and then hanging him again, placing the rope around prisoners' necks and then pushing away the stool on which they stood, trampling to death a young Jewish prisoner, shooting others in the stomach—and all that for years, because Hitler wanted it that way. The same Kaduk moved to West Berlin in

1956 and became a male nurse in the municipal administration of Willi Brandt. Today his patients sent letters to the court in Frankfurt to testify that he was a good, a warmhearted, a caring nurse. In the hospital he was known as Papa Kaduk.

Again my astonishment. So this is what man is? This is what it means to be a man? Or might it be regret, atonement, internal reversal, death of the old Adam? The way Kaduk sat next to his lawyer, broad, massive, and self-assured, a fat, no-neck butcher type who knew how to stand up for himself, he did not give this impression. He was just the old Adam, who could not recall a thing. And if one day they hadn't come to fetch him from his hospital, he would probably have died in Berlin at the age of seventy or eighty, an old and deserving citizen who would have been awarded his pension and some plaque of recognition or other—a citizen of the free world.

For the first time I began to understand why there are Jews who refuse to return to this second German republic though it has become decent and bearable once more. Fear, a very personal fear—the streetcar conductor, the man behind the counter at the post office or the railroad station, the druggist, or precisely this competent male nurse from West Berlin—of course, all of them could have been the one. You can never be sure, New York or Tel Aviv is safer in that respect, and someone who has no business in our country but to mourn the dead—isn't it reasonable, isn't it unavoidable that he has this small, private, deathly fear of us Germans?

The voice had been coming over the loudspeaker again for the last ten minutes. In the meantime I had learned that it belonged to the first prosecution witness, the first witness of the hundred and fifty who would follow. The witness's name was Dr. Wolken. He was a physician from Vienna, a white-haired older man whose movements seemed somewhat stiff and rigid. He was severely disabled. He too had survived, he too had adapted again, he too had become a citizen of his country once more, a man with a family, friends, fellow workers—tormentor and victim both survived. Their survival and their confrontation were the prerequisites of this trial. What separated them today was chiefly the psychology of memory, the mechanism of forgetting. The one group wanted to forget but could not. The others were supposed to remember but could not. They had forgotten everything; they planted radishes and established nursery schools and engaged in sports. I did not know which was more tormenting, remembering or forgetting. Freud taught us that guilt can never be forgotten, only repressed, and that repression leads to neuroses and compulsions. But was Freud correct in the face of Mulka and others? Where were the neuroses? And was there really redemption in bringing the past to consciousness, articulating it? Was the process not simply another torture of experience? I heard the voice again. "A group of ninety children arrived. They were kept in the quarantine camp for several days. Then trucks came, and they were loaded on them to be driven to the gas chambers. There was one, a slightly older boy, who called to the children when they resisted, 'Just get in the car, please don't cry. You've seen how your parents and grandparents were gassed. We'll see them again up there.' And then the boy turned to the SS men and shouted, 'But don't you ever believe that you'll get away with it. You'll perish the same way you are making us perish.'" After a pause the voice from the loudspeaker adds, "He was a courageous boy. In this instant he said what he had to say."

It was an agonizing moment. The clock in the chamber showed 11:37. But was that the correct time? Hadn't time stopped for a moment here in this chamber? It was one of those times when a court was no longer a court, when the walls opened, when it became the tribunal of the century. It was not, now, a matter of all these petty villains, the Mulkas and Bogers and Kaduks. Here history was being witnessed, history was being written, inventory was being taken, testimony was being given of the dance of death in the twentieth century. The actors in the horror show were gathered, the tormentors and the victims. They were to confront each other here, to bear witness to what had passed, to tell the world what had happened once upon a time.

And this too happened: "There were many naked women who, after a sorting-out process, had been flogged up onto a truck and then driven to the gas chambers. We were standing roll call in front of the barracks, and they shouted over to us men, they hoped for help from us ... we were their natural protectors. But we just stood there trembling—we could not help. Then the trucks drove off, and the wagon with the red cross followed at the end of each column. But it held no sick people, it carried the poison gas."

I looked around the hall. Everywhere embarrassed expressions, uneasy silence, German awkwardness—at last. To the left sat the journalists, writing along as if under a spell. Also to the left, in the gallery, sat the spectators. Every morning, well before eight o'clock, they stood in line in a side street to get the few entrance tickets. Who were they? What German came here of his own free will? They had good, hopeful faces, a great deal of youth—students and schoolchildren, attending with speechless astonishment a spectacle allegedly staged by their parents. Their parents? Oh, no, surely not theirs, but surely other parents. My parents? Oh, no, surely not mine, but surely other parents. There were a few old people as well, sixty or seventy years old, and you could tell by looking at them that it was not a craving for sensationalism that brought them. What was missing was my generation, the middle generation, those who were surely concerned, who were surely there. But they did not want to know anything about it now; they knew it all already, they were familiar with it. Right now—just before noon—they had to be at work, had to make money, had to keep the economic miracle rolling. He who looks back is lost.

To the right of me sat three nuns, girlishly slim and prematurely aged. They must be Protestants from Darmstadt, Sisters of Mary, members of a religious community founded after the war and dedicated to expiating the Christian sin against the Jews. They always sent some of their members so that they might know what to pray for. They were typical of a new, modern church. Right now, were the Sisters of Mary praying for the naked women on the truck? Did prayer help in such a situation? Did judges' sentences and judgments help? Could anything help? I did not know—I of all people did not know. I only knew suddenly that I really was attending the Auschwitz trials and that it was a good thing I came.

For this was the way it was sure to go on: for

223

weeks, for months, perhaps for years. Hundreds of people would come to this court, from America and Israel, from Canada and England; all the scattered children of this dead city would come together to create a mosaic, tile by tile, of their small, fragmented prison world. They would expose a labyrinth of guilt from which there was no escape. The labyrinth would be horribly confusing and would destroy all self-righteousness, all arrogance, all clarity of distance.

There would be witnesses here who would intercede for SS officers with appreciation, even with gratitude. Such things did happen. There were some wearers of the death's head who behaved fairly and courageously and who said, I prefer not to. As a result of prisoners' testimony, they were set free soon after the end of the war. And there were some prisoners, often people persecuted on political grounds, who gained power in the camps, who became trustees, and who engaged in more beating, torturing, and killing than many a man in uniform. For example, the man to the right of me.

Bedenarek, Emil, merchant, not an SS man but one of Hitler's victims, accused here of having tortured fellow prisoners to death while he was a block captain and a political prisoner in protective custody. "In numerous instances he allegedly forced prisoners of the penal company to remain under the cold shower until they were chilled, numbed, and unable to stand." One of Hitler's victims in search of his own victims.

"Thereupon the accused is alleged to have ordered them carried out into the courtyard of the penal block, where they remained lying through the night, so that most of them died. The accused is alleged to have especially distinguished himself in the summer of 1944 during the liquidation of Family Camp B IIb by joining with various SS troops in beating Jewish prisoners who resisted transport to the gas chamber. In this action at least ten prisoners lost their lives." And the indictment against Emil Bedenarek, who today owned his own business as well as a station restaurant, was not finished yet. One of Hitler's victims, himself a murderer.

That was the labyrinth of Auschwitz. No, there really was not a great deal of truth to the rumor that this new wave of trials was playing at denazification, that they represented a search for scapegoats, belated revenge on the SS, a witch hunt for petty Nazis. The question of political orientation and organization did not arise at all. It was simply a matter of murder. Even Jews could become criminals, and occasionally members of the SS could become resistance fighters.

For the death camp was not only a political nightmare, it was also a social reality, an extra-world with new hierarchies and privileges and new forms of oppression and favoritism. The reasons for your being there might vary; but once you were in it, you had joined this new, second world, the separate order of the camp where, according to new laws, you could rise or sink once more. And who wanted to sink?

I remembered film strips from the Warsaw Ghetto; they showed Jews, emaciated Jewish policemen with armbands, hitting their coreligionists with clubs, hoping thus to find favor with the SS. The SS did not care to dirty its own hands. In Germany, too, there were Jewish councils that were sensible, conciliatory, and prudent and that as late as 1938 told the members of their congregations, Surely you can understand, it's reasonable, we have to let them register us, we can't help being Jews, it doesn't mean anything. And I heard about trials in Israel where to this day Jews are sentenced because they were the most feared bullies in the whole camp.

Here in Frankfurt, at 87 Unterlindau, a lawyer and notary who was an SS judge was in practice today. When he visited Auschwitz in those days and saw the hell there, he began to indict the torturers one by one. His name was Dr. Morgen, and he would not be testifying until later on in the trials, but it was already clear that one SS officer had the courage to proceed legally against other SS officers. Sentences of up to twelve years in the penitentiary were handed down. It was even claimed that in 1943 this man initiated criminal proceedings against the camp commander, Höss, before the SS Court in Weimar; but of course nothing came of it. A subject for Ionesco or another playwright of the absurd: SS justice engages in the highly embarrassing exercise of trying cases of prisoner maltreatment in Auschwitz—a violation of the Führer's decree. Penitentiary sentences were dispensed even as the crematoriums burned brightly day and night—not a violation of the Führer's decree. But no, it was not a trendy plot device in the theater of the absurd. It was the reality of those days.

Noontime. The presiding officer had already given several searching glances at the large wall clock, where the hands stood at just before twelve thirty. Noontime. Time to go home. Everywhere in Germany workers were dropping their tools and sitting down to steaming bowls of soup, to casseroles redolent of cabbage, to roasts—all washed down with beer. Here we would do the same, of course.

"The court is in recess until two o'clock," I heard the presiding officer say, and everyone breathed a sigh of relief, rose, was suddenly in a hurry. Each person wanted to get to his car, his

227

tram, his table in the restaurant, or his couch at home—a vacation from Auschwitz, a two-hour reprieve from history. Only to get out of this ghostly labyrinth, out into a bit of the palpable, harmless reality of our country. Now there was a crowd at the coat room, pushing and shoving. Of course we were still a little clumsy and benumbed, as after an absorbing play. We rushed down the halls, coattails fluttering.

Ahead of me walked Breitwieser, the intellectual-looking bookkeeper who was an expert on Cyclon B. He walked quickly and with a springy step, but on the stairs he limped a little. Where might he be going? For a moment I was obsessed with the idea of following him, observing the car he would get into, and with whom he would spend his lunch hour. I wondered: What kind of figure would he cut among the other Germans? Would they notice anything in the restaurant while he sat and ate? Would he be conspicuous in any way? I should check it out. But then I knew that it would be quite fruitless. People who were experts on Cyclon B ate and slept and loved just like anybody else in this country. They were contemporaries, fellows in the sick German epoch.

Difficult to find the way back now. Nothing from before held true; it was only the present. The sun shone brightly on the Römerplatz, and it was as warm as spring and as bright as Milan or Turin at this time of year. Tourists with their cameras sauntered across the cobbled square and snapped a few pictures in passing. "Lovely," an old lady next to me said. A group of blacks examining a fountain was amazed by remnants of the Middle Ages—the wonder of tourists, lasting all of thirty seconds. A half-timbered building dating from 1383 glittered in the background, freshly varnished—the famous Gate House No. 1, Frankfurt's oldest building. Could you help loving this homey, dreamy Germany of nooks and crannies? Joyce and Thomas Wolfe once stood in this square while Hitler ruled over Germany—intoxicated and enthralled by German Gothic.

I walked over to Saint Paul's Cathedral and crossed Saint Paul's Square. All at once the racing, hastening noontime traffic of a living German metropolis beat against me. It was like a hurricane of technology; I felt lost in it. Now it was impossible to think of shooting and gassing, of chimneys and crematoriums; it took all my attention just to get across the street safely. The area was dangerous, like a civilized jungle, a battle of machines—long ribbons of cars, signals, signs, green lights and red lights and the yellow blinkers of the turn signals, policemen waving their arms like dolls. You shoved and pushed and waited, and someone shouted something at a driver who did not move quickly enough on the green, and the shouter pointed at his own forehead with his index finger. That's how it was. That was Frankfurt at 12:25, commercial center of the free Germany; that was the Federal Republic at noontime. All the drivers seemed to belong to the same age group—men in their mid-forties, now playing at war on the street, in business, on the stock exchange. That was Germany—its other, second, competent face. You must not think of Auschwitz. They'd kill you with their cars.

I took refuge in a side street. Abruptly paralyzed by melancholy, I crept past walls. Here too nothing but tall, new buildings, but then it grew more quiet; large, cared-for bookstores appeared, and suddenly a brown, tall, patrician house with bull's-eye windowpanes and staggered floors and cast-iron doors told me that I was near the birthplace of German classicism, the Goethe House. Two American sightseeing busses were parked in the narrow street, spewing out tourists who wanted a quick chance to wrap themselves around the Germany of the poets and thinkers. They'd fall for the package, I thought: Goethe's junk, Frau Rath's frying pan, nothing but trash, nothing but gimcrack. The real Goethe House was destroyed in the war, burned out. The Goethe House no longer existed. Goethe and classicism were finished in Germany. It had to mean something that during the worst years of Auschwitz this house too turned to ashes.

Later I sat in a small Rumanian restaurant not far from the Goethe House. Refined silence. Only nine or ten tables, along the wall a long board with fancy appetizers, muted music in the background. The owner himself came over—an older, white-haired man from Bucharest—and in broken German, with much bowing and a little French, he recommended the specialties of his establishment. And I thought, What is it about us Germans? Are we once more the masters of Europe? Now the same people whom only yesterday we attacked, plundered, oppressed, and tried to turn into slave races are falling all over themselves to please us, to serve us. Really they should hate us, should despise us, should shun us everywhere, but they do nothing of the sort. They come to our country; millions of foreign workers live among us; and millions of Germans vacation in their countries. Have we, then, become a new, a better people?

I opened the newspaper and nervously scanned the headlines. I read, "Too Much Gold." Wait a minute—could I have got that one right? Did it really say something about too much gold? And I began to read the item in earnest. "West Germany's Gold Administrator is complaining of a condition that almost all the world's governments ardently long for: in the vaults of the Federal Bank, gold is again piling up." I continued reading that today, February 27, the gold reserves in Frankfurt ran to 30.3 billion marks. "The Federal Republic estimates that during the past 12 months more than 2 billion marks in foreign capital flowed into West Germany. As much as 25 percent of all German loans during the year were acquired by foreign investors." And I asked myself again, What is it about this Germany?

Since it would probably be awhile before my dinner arrived, I took out the notes I had jotted down earlier, during the witness's testimony. I only wrote a few words—words of the witness, Dr. Wolken, not SS words but words of the victim, language of the camp. I read: switch off; launch; liquidate; load; gas; perish; select; work up equipment; work off accumulating corpses; go into the gas; Women's Camp B I: Cyclon B; go to the platform; lead off; turn off; forwarding; transferring; roll call; exercising; running; shooting; loading; dousing; orchestra; sound of waltz music; canine patrol; rabbit chase; beatings; inscribed in the death ledger; switch off Moslems; cart off Moslems; kill Moslems; inject into the heart muscle; break the spinal column; hopping ..."

As I scanned these phrases, my dream of the previous night suddenly became clear. Of course, that was the language of the old uniform, that was the word *Sanka*, which I could not remember. This language was still alive, still existed; here in Frankfurt it was stirring again. We could put on as many new uniforms, as many golden garments as we liked. The staff sergeant who yelled at me and refused me a new uniform was Hitler, of course; he still lived in us as well. He still ruled in the dark, underground; somehow he had made a crack in all of us. Some chased after money and others attended the Auschwitz trials, some covered up and others uncovered. These were two sides of the same German coin. This Hitler, I thought, remains with us—all the days of our lives.

Afterword: Ten Years Later

I wrote this book in the winter of 1964–65, and it was first published in 1966. Did I really write it? Did it not rather write itself? It was a beginning, a start, a first attempt to gain my own freedom.

Such attempts, especially when they are not undertaken at an advanced age, always have a coercive and explosive nature. They pour forth as if they were dictated. Compulsion is at work, an unconscious dynamic, the urge to finally free oneself of a heavy burden. This burden is called the past, youth, the trauma of childhood—a very personal and at the same time a political story. At the outset one is reluctant to write. What one wants to do is save oneself from unbearable systemic pressures. The odd thing about literature is that such personal salvation manages to save others as well. In this sense, *A Crack in the Wall* was an unqualified success. Critics and readers welcomed it. Except for a few voices on the political right and the left, it was greeted with unanimous praise at the time.

The book has its own history, which now, in retrospect, deserves to be mentioned. It was not really planned; it wrote itself rather unexpectedly, from the end to the beginning. In the mid-1960s I moved from Baden-Baden to Frankfurt on the Main. I emerged from a long period of silence—merely oppressive toward the end, marked by inner confusion and professional dependence—to embark on the life of a freelance writer. It was a time of expectations, of curiosity, of hope.

In those days Frankfurt offered a great deal of material for contemporaries interested in social criticism. Among the people I came to know was the Hessian chief state counselor, since deceased but not forgotten, who was then in the process of preparing for the Auschwitz trials. Fritz Bauer became my friend, and he invited me to attend the trials. For four weeks I sat as a silent witness in the courtroom, and afterward I wrote a series of articles for the magazine *Monat*; subsequently, somewhat expanded and revised, they became the final chapter of *A Crack in the Wall*.

Only later, in the autumn of 1964, did my own memories slowly rise to the surface. When a writer attends a trial, can he ever identify with anyone other than the defendant? In view of the monstrosities under consideration at the Auschwitz trials, the psychology of such a reaction may seem absurd—it was at work all the same. The bestiality

revealed there could not prevent me from asking,
And you? How would you have acted in those days
if you had accidentally found yourself, a lowly
soldier, in the bureaucracy of this death camp? Are
there born murderers, or aren't all of them produced by society? How much would you have
accepted silently? How guilty would you have
become? True, there is a threshold of murder—
but where exactly is your limit? Retrospectively,
then, it was I who was being examined during the
trial; the proceedings were directed against me as
well.

Repeatedly the critical reception of *A Crack in
the Wall* testified to the radical morality of its way
of thinking. Marcel Reich-Ranicki, writing in *Die
Zeit*, called the book "a Germany without lies." If
such should be the case, it is due, as I realize today,
to precisely this drastic, even self-torturing act of
identification with the world of the accused. I did
not exclude myself, I did not remove myself, I was
not content with outrage. I was obsessed with the
question of my own past.

National Socialist fanaticism was certainly
not to be found in the teenager from a petit-
bourgeois Berlin family. On the contrary, within
the limits of his modest opportunities, he always
disengaged himself and was even able to place into
evidence a few undeniable though fruitless acts of
political resistance. But was that enough? Were

there not, beyond guilt and atonement, universal erroneous attitudes that furnished the preconditions for Hitler's dictatorship in Germany?

I began to remember, to trace the way back, to enter into a past. I returned to my youth and my childhood. You could call it my first travel experience: a journey into my own past. I thereupon found that the first chapter, "A Place Like Eichkamp," started to take shape. I rediscovered my parents' home, my youth under Hitler—a wholly atypical, unique youth. Precisely because there was no need to embellish my own guilt, because I and my family had never been in thrall to the German enthusiasm for Hitler, an ideal, uncomplicated opportunity for self-analysis presented itself. I stumbled upon something I had not really been conscious of before—the phenomenon of the unpolitical German petit bourgeoisie, which in its social insecurity, its instability and need for the irrational, furnished the fertile ground for the internal seizure of power by National Socialism.

Thus, step by step, the four central chapters describing my development up to the end of the war came into being. A further chapter, intended to relate my wartime experiences as a German private first class between 1941 and 1945—which should by rights come between "In Custody" and "1945: Zero Hour"—refused time and again to let itself be written. My participation in the army and the war took place, as it were, outside my ego experience. To this day I have not been able to make them properly my own. The critical reader cannot help but find a gap here, one to which I readily confess.

Instead, the theme of family kept thrusting itself even more insistently to the forefront. In the process, my parents' home became, almost unintentionally, a metaphor for Germany. The title, which I chose deliberately and which in some quarters aroused skeptical opposition, is precisely my theme: I am not speaking of a smashed, destroyed, divided house—rather it collapsed from internal rot, just as the "collapse" of Germany occurred, not in 1945, but in 1933, from the inside out. To that extent the chapter "Requiem for Ursula" is the key to my overall theme. It describes the physical dissolution of a German family—which cannot be entirely grasped through reason—its inner process of decay, its unconscious sympathy with death. My vision of myself as the last, the only survivor—which, I believe, can be recognized in my subsequent books as well—had its origin in that event, and it has never left me. It still determines my being. Of course the more hospitable, more productive phrase "The last are free" also applies. This is the freedom in which I live today.

Books, it is a well-known fact, have lives of their own. Even as the public begins to pay attention to one, its author, freed from the problems it presented, has already moved away from it. That has been true since the time of Goethe's *Werther*. Someone writes about suicide, not in order to kill himself, but in order to go on living. Someone writes about the end, not in order to die, but in order to find a new beginning. So it was in this case as well. I felt freed once I had finished the manuscript.

In the years that followed, I began to come to terms with the world around me through critical writings on contemporary subjects—concrete confrontations with the Germany of the late Adenauer period, with East Germany, with the division of Germany, and later with "foreign homelands," as one of my books was called—journeys into the world with the baggage of the past. Whether this is to be seen as an enlargement of my horizons or rather, as has occasionally been suggested, as an attenuation of my original inspiration, I do not want to decide here. I have never felt the two "modes of travel" to be contradictory. For me, both have been necessary and unavoidable stages in my growth.

As an author, one can only find oneself by entering into the world. But one can only set out for this world if one has first come to terms with oneself. The value I assign to self-cleansing, to cleaning house, seems to me not to have changed in the course of my life. The message of the key sentence in this book, at the very end—"This Hitler, I think, remains with us—all the days of our lives"—still holds true and is manifest in my later publications. To that extent I feel I have remained true to *A Crack in the Wall*.

Of course ten years later one can see more clearly the strengths and weaknesses of such an initial attempt. Quite inescapably it bears the stamp of a work produced in the mode of Storm and Stress. It draws its power of persuasion from an originality of questioning, even a naïveté, that we possess only once in our lives—at the very beginning. Subjectivity sets the tone. An adolescent obstinacy dominates, forcing to the background the stylistic irony that clearly seems natural to me. A psychoanalytical interpretation might detect an anal-aggressive confrontation in the obstinacy phase, but such psychologically apt formulations contribute remarkably little to explaining the events narrated.

Nevertheless, on some pages I now sense an antagonism that, as in the portrait of my parents, borders on injustice, even unkindness. Today I would tell some things with more discrimination, adducing more levels of psychological complexity. At times the prose seems driven by emotional dramatizing that is not entirely free of a hidden joy in exhibitionism, but this underlying narcissism—

that is, the tendency to please oneself—is unpremeditated, totally naïve. Today I would try through deliberate irony to reflect it in the narrative process. Even after ten years, the language radiates an intensity that seems to me to remain fresh, but now and again, by contemporary standards, it is too direct, too massive, too oversimplified, in the manner of a woodcut. Today I would take greater pains to represent the difficulty of various issues. Thus revised, the work would be fairer, but surely it would lose an element of passion and vitality.

The fact that pain is a powerful but by no means a sufficient signpost for a writer seems to me, in rereading the book, demonstrated on many a page. All the same, my painful start brings to the surface so much social and communal reality that I thought it worthwhile—even politically desirable—to issue a new edition of the book, which has gone out of print. The generation of those who were spectators, collaborators, opponents—in any case, contemporaries—of Hitler is beginning to thin out. The moment is in sight when few if any eyewitnesses to those twelve years will be left. Today's history books, monographs, and texts furnish evidence of what there is to be taught and learned about the era, but the private failures, the personal attitudes, and the social climate of those days between the shifting, murderous rocks of history cannot be captured in history books. The human fresco serving as the background of events requires personal reminiscence and literary presentation.

Unaltered by ten years of growth, I submit: The book contains authentic news from a realm that, already submerged, must never be forgotten. It contains the experiences of a generation, which can be helpful to new generations insofar as they are eager to learn how it really was, this business of Hitler and the Germans. For that reason validity continues to attach to Wolfgang Köppen's statement on the original publication of *A Crack in the Wall*: "Thus Krüger's look back in anger and sorrow could and should become a German household guide in the good traditional sense of someone's having written down and preserved what happened to a nation."

I reread the text for the new German edition. Except for a few allusions that were appropriate at the time but have since been superseded, I have changed nothing.

Horst Krüger
Frankfurt am Main
March 1976